P9-CFP-101

THE AMERICAN BAR ASSOCIATION

GUIDE TO
HOME
OWNERSHIP

Other Books by the American Bar Association

The American Bar Association Family Legal Guide

THE AMERICAN BAR ASSOCIATION

GUIDE TO
HOME
OWNERSHIP

THE COMPLETE AND EASY GUIDE
TO ALL THE LAW
EVERY HOME OWNER SHOULD KNOW

TIMES ᴛ BOOKS

RANDOM HOUSE

Points of view or opinions in this publication do not necessarily represent the official policies or positions of the American Bar Association.

This book is not a substitute for an attorney, nor does it attempt to answer all questions about all situations you may encounter.

Copyright © 1995 by the American Bar Association

All rights reserved under International and Pan-American Copyright Conventions. Published in the United States by Random House, Inc., New York, and simultaneously in Canada by Random House of Canada Limited, Toronto.

Library of Congress Cataloging-in-Publication Data

The American Bar Association guide to home ownership : the complete and easy guide to all the law every home owner should know.
    p.   cm.
  Includes bibliographical references and index.
  ISBN 0-8129-2535-1
  1. Home ownership—Law and legislation—United States—Popular works. 2. Home owners—United States—Handbooks, manuals, etc. I. American Bar Association.
KF390.H53A46   1995
349.73'02464—dc20
[347.3002464]   94-40827

Manufactured in the United States of America on acid-free paper
68975

FOREWORD

■

HILARIE BASS, *Chair*
ABA Standing Committee on Public Education

THE LAW AFFECTS each of us in our daily lives—when we send our kids to school, take the car in for repair, use a credit card, make a purchase, or go to work. If we don't understand how law governs our rights and responsibilities, we're at a considerable disadvantage in today's America.

That is the purpose of *The American Bar Association Legal Guides*—to explain the law to you in simple, easy-to-understand language. These books use concise, straightforward language. By avoiding legal jargon and technicalities, they discuss in everyday words how the law affects you at home, at work, and at play. Best of all, these books will help you to avoid legal problems, to identify those that you may have, and to determine which legal problems you can solve on your own and which require the assistance of an attorney.

These books help you understand the important legal issues about marriage, separation, and divorce. They explore the legal aspects of owning a home, and the world of contracts, big and little. They tell you what you need to know to plan your estate *and* save money for yourself and your loved ones. They even provide guidance on planning for disability, and on end-of-life issues.

These books are organized so you can easily find what you need to know. Brief articles giving additional information on topics of great interest appear alongside the text. You will also find information about state laws, as well as about federal laws that apply across the United States.

No book can answer all the questions you might have on the law. To help you find additional help, sections at the end of each book tell you where to get more information. These sections refer you to many free or inexpensive publications, and suggest services that government agencies, bar associations, and other groups can provide at either minimal or no cost.

When reading *The American Bar Association Legal Guides*, please keep some important points in mind. First, these books cannot and do not pretend to provide legal advice—only a lawyer who understands the facts of your particular case can do that. Although every effort has been made to present material that is as up-to-date as possible, laws can and do change.

Thus, these books should be considered an introduction to the law in each area. They are not the final word. If you are thinking about pursuing any legal action, consult first with a lawyer, bar association, or lawyer referral service to assure yourself of knowledgeable assistance. Armed with the knowledge and insights provided in *The American Bar Association Legal Guides*, you can be confident that the legal decisions you make will be in your best interests.

Hilarie Bass is in private practice in Miami, Florida. She is president of the Florida Bar Foundation and a past member of the Board of Governors of the American Bar Association.

FOREWORD

Gurden Buck
Robinson & Cole
Hartford, Connecticut

Bernice Cilley
Mays & Valentine
Richmond, Virginia

Martha Easter-Wells
Attorney at Law
Davenport, Iowa

Edward T. Flynn
Attorneys' Title Guaranty
   Fund, Inc.
Chicago, Illinois

Sally H. Foote
Thompson & Foote
Clearwater, Florida

Richard M. Frome
Attorney at Law
New York, New York

Jerry T. Gorman
Attorneys' Title Guaranty
   Fund, Inc.
Champaign, Illinois

Leonard M. Groupe
Groupe & Katz
Chicago, Illinois

David L. Haron
Frank & Stefani
Troy, Michigan

John Horwich
University of Montana
   School of Law
Missoula, Montana

Jonathan Hoyt
Attorney at Law
Clinton, Connecticut

Eric Larsen
Attorney at Law
Sacramento, California

Ronald Jay Maas
Weichert Realtors
Morris Plains, New Jersey

Amy Meland
Attorneys' Title Guaranty
   Fund, Inc.
Chicago, Illinois

Frank A. Melchior
1st American Title Ins. Co.
Iselin, New Jersey

Steven Paul
Warner & Stackpoll
Boston, Massachusetts

Leopold Z. Sher
McGlinchey, Stafford & Lang
New Orleans, Louisiana

Julius J. Zschau
Baynard, Harrell, Ostow &
   Ulrich, P.A.
Clearwater, Florida

PREFACE

■

ROBERT A. STEIN, *Executive Director*
American Bar Association

THE AMERICAN BAR ASSOCIATION LEGAL
GUIDES are designed to provide guidance for people on
important legal questions they encounter in everyday life. When
American families are asked to describe their legal needs, the topics that come up repeatedly are housing, personal finance, family
and domestic concerns (usually in conjunction with divorce and
child support), wills and estates, and employment-related issues.
In addition, more and more Americans have questions about operating a business, often out of the home.

These are the topics that *The American Bar Association Legal
Guides* cover in plain, direct language. We have made a special
effort to make the books practical, by using situations and problems you are likely to encounter. The goal of these books is to
give helpful information on a range of options that can be used in
solving everyday legal problems, so that you can make informed
decisions on how best to handle your particular question.

The American Bar Association wants Americans to be aware
of the full range of options available when they are confronted
with a problem that might have a "legal" solution. The Association has supported programs to eliminate delay in the courts,
and has worked to promote fast, affordable alternatives to lawsuits, such as mediation, arbitration, conciliation, and small
claims court. Through ABA support for lawyer referral programs
and pro bono services (where lawyers donate their time), people
have been able to find the best lawyer for their particular case
and have received quality legal help within their budget.

The American Bar Association Legal Guides discuss all these alternatives, suggesting the wide range of options open to you. We hope that they will help you feel more comfortable with the law and will remove much of the mystery from the legal system.

Several hundred members of the Association have contributed to *The American Bar Association Legal Guides*—as authors and as reviewers who have guaranteed the guides' accuracy. To them—and to the ABA's Standing Committee on Public Education, which was the primary force behind the publications—I express my thanks and gratitude, and that of the Association and of lawyers everywhere.

Robert A. Stein is executive director of the American Bar Association. He was formerly dean of the University of Minnesota Law School.

PREFACE

CONTENTS

INTRODUCTION

IT'S THE AMERICAN DREAM! A home of your own. It may be perched alone on a hilltop, tucked into a suburban cul-de-sac, or hidden above the bustling energy of the city. It may be a cozy little Cape Cod, a massive log cabin, or perhaps a brand-new high-rise condo. Whatever you've chosen, one of the best things about it is that it's yours.

The dream of home ownership is still a driving force in America. According to a 1993 survey by the Federal National Mortgage Association, owning a home is a goal so important to most Americans that they're willing to make major tradeoffs to achieve it. Of the 1,521 people surveyed, four out of five reported that they would rather own their own home than take a better job in a city where they could only afford to rent. Two out of three said they would be willing to work a second job if that was the only way they could afford to own their own home. Four out of five said they would rather own a home and have a long commute from work than rent a place nearby.

There's more to owning a home, though, than saving up for a down payment. Just as a house has a frame to support the walls and keep the roof overhead, it also has a legal framework of rights and duties that can keep your dream of property ownership from crashing in on your head.

This book is designed to help you understand that legal framework, and to answer some questions you might have. What legal form of ownership is best for your circumstances? What can happen if you don't have clear title to your property? What's the legal status of condominium declarations, bylaws, and restrictions? Who's liable if someone gets hurt on your property?

This book can also help you avoid legal problems and work through other kinds of problems that might arise. How can you handle disputes with your neighbors? What can you do to avoid problems with your remodeling contractor? How can you protect your property from burglars? What tax breaks are available for home owners? What are your options if you can't make the mortgage payments?

The law is constantly changing, so no book can promise to give you authoritative advice guaranteed to fit your circumstances. But this guide can help you understand how the law may affect you and when you may want to consult a lawyer.

If you do need to find a lawyer, ask for recommendations from people whose judgment you respect. For routine matters involving home ownership you probably don't need the best-known, most expensive lawyer in town. Your local or state bar association can refer you to an attorney with expertise in the area that concerns you.

When you go for an initial consultation (which in many cases is free of charge), take along any documents that you think might be helpful. Jot down names, dates, and other information pertaining to the matter. Think about what you'd like to accomplish. A good lawyer will explain your options, what each is likely to cost, and your chances for success. But it's up to you to decide what to do.

Be sure you understand the fee arrangement—whether your lawyer will charge a flat fee for this matter, an hourly fee (how much per hour?), or a contingent fee (usually reserved for litigation) of a certain percentage of whatever you win in court. Find out who will be working on the file, because less-experienced associates usually rate a lower hourly fee. Then ask what you can track down yourself to help use your attorney's time most efficiently.

We at the ABA hope this book will help you understand your home's legal framework, avoid legal troubles, save money, and enjoy that special place that you call home.

THE AMERICAN BAR ASSOCIATION

GUIDE TO
HOME
OWNERSHIP

■

CHAPTER ONE

Home Ownership 101

A Guide to What Your Deed Really Means

YOUR OWN HOME! It's your little starter house, your grand Victorian, your mountain hideaway, your suburban townhouse. After years of renting and saving and dreaming, you've bought a home and it's yours.

Now what do you need to know, to make sure you can keep right on enjoying that special home? Certainly, if you don't already know how to start a reluctant lawn mower, change a faucet washer, fix a broken windowpane, and cope with rising water in the basement, you'd better be prepared to learn.

But there are a few legal matters you'll want to understand right away to make sure your ownership of the home means what you think it does. This chapter will give you a basic introduction to the law of home ownership, including rights and possible restrictions. Note that the laws of each state govern the ownership of property within state borders, so the general principles that follow are only intended to give you an idea of the options that may be available and what they might mean to you.

CHECK THAT DEED

Begin by checking the way your ownership is described on the deed, because the wording may have serious ramifications years from now. Make sure the deed says what you want it to.

Although a deed almost never mentions the house or other structures standing on a property, it provides an exact description of its location and boundaries. If there's any question about where the boundaries lie, you can usually resolve the question through a survey or by talking things out with your neighbors. See the section on boundary lines in chapter 7, "Love Your Neighbor?"

Although property buyers tend to focus on how big their property is and where its boundaries lie, two other items on the deed have far-reaching implications: the form of ownership and the way it's shared among owners.

Forms of Ownership

Let's start with the forms of home ownership, which have to do with how long the title is valid. These days, the most common form of ownership is **fee simple**. It's also the most complete form, because, in theory, titles in fee simple are valid forever, unlike some of the older forms, such as an **estate for years**, where the title reverts to the former owner at some specified time. People who own property in a fee simple form may sell it, rent it out, transfer it to their heirs, and to some extent limit its use in the future.

The term *fee simple* comes from feudal England, where a noble landholder would grant an estate, called a fee, to a faithful subject in exchange for service or money. In the thirteenth century the grant would normally be a **life estate**, which meant that when the tenant died the land would revert to the lord. But if the lord intended for the tenant to be able to keep the estate in the family after he died, he'd include the phrase "and his heirs" in the legal document. That's still the phrase to include on a deed if the owner is to hold the property in fee simple, able to sell it or bequeath it.

It remains possible to transfer property as a life estate, but doing so is not common. The form allows owner A to bequeath the house to B, say his wife, until she dies, then to C, their child. People used to do that to avoid estate taxes, but there's no need now that the marital tax deduction protects property bequeathed by one's spouse from estate taxes. Some people still use the form to retain their homestead exemption without having the property tied up in probate when they die, or to give title to a descendant who may better qualify for financing, while retaining an assured roof over their heads.

A life estate severely restricts the new owner's ability to sell the property. If Mrs. Smith has a life estate in her home, she'd likely have trouble selling it because the title would no longer be valid when she died. If you want to give a house to your elderly parents until they die and then have it go to your children, it makes more sense either to set up a trust to that effect, or to provide in your will that they may stay there as long as they live. Consult an estate planning attorney on how to accomplish your goals while avoiding legal pitfalls.

Joint Ownership

The other critical aspect of a deed is who's named as the owner, and, if there's more than one owner, precisely how ownership is shared.

If you're a single home owner living alone, the ownership is probably very simple. Your name may well be the only one on the deed unless, for example, you bought the house with your parents in order to qualify for a loan, or your ex-spouse is still a co-owner.

When there's more than one owner, ownership can get complicated. The form of ownership listed on the deed really makes a difference. Long-term implications include who can transfer interests to someone else, how much of the property is available to one owner's creditors, whether the property goes through probate when one party dies, and whether the surviving owner faces a whopping tax on capital gain when it's time to sell the property. It's important to think about what you want the deed to accomplish and to take the necessary steps to get it precisely in writing and properly filed.

Unmarried co-owners have to choose whether to be **tenants in common** or **joint tenants with right of survivorship**. Married co-owners could choose either of those forms, or in some states might opt to be **tenants by the entirety** or in others to hold their home as **community property**.

Let's take a look at an imaginary couple facing these choices. To see the full range of options we'll make them married, because while married couples can choose either form available to unmarried co-owners, in most states at least one form is available to married couples only.

Suppose that Bob and Susan Smith are buying a split-level house in Gainesville, Florida. It's their first house, and they aren't sure how to title it. What are their options?

• **One Name Only.** Bob's kind of a traditional guy. He's the one who earned the money they used to buy the house, so why not put just his name on the deed? That was common practice fifty years ago—and you can bet the one name wasn't the wife's. The custom of the property being in the husband's name was especially hard on wives before the marital deduction, because wives inheriting property from their husbands would sometimes have to sell the property to pay estate taxes on it.

These days, one of the chief concerns when considering property ownership in a single name is liability for court judgments. Suppose Bob insists on titling the house in his name alone. A few years later he's driving home from an office party, swerves into the wrong lane and causes a horrible car crash. He lands in court, where the judge assesses a hefty judgment against him—and his insurance won't cover it. Because the house legally belongs only to him, in most states it could be sold to cover the judgment.

Living in Florida, Bob and Susan would be better off than most. Twenty-two states offer some protection through their **homestead exemption**, which allows people subject to big judgments (or going bankrupt) to keep a small house to live in. But the maximum lot size and value may be quite small—such as, in Arkansas, a quarter acre and $2,500 value. Florida's homestead exemption places no limit on the home's value.

If Bob were a doctor with no malpractice insurance, he might want to avoid the risk of losing the house because of a judgment against him by putting the house in Susan's name (or vice versa, if she were the doctor). Some people do that. But they should consult an attorney about all the aspects of their situation, including whether such ownership would accomplish that purpose, and the tax implications, before making their decision.

• **Tenants in Common.** If Bob and Susan decide to own their home as tenants in common, they're each considered the owner of an undivided interest in the whole property. They each own half of the value of the house (unless the deed specifies a different proportion), but it's not as if Susan owned the north half and Bob owned the south. They may each sell their interest to someone else or leave it to someone in their will, whether or not the other approves. If they couldn't agree on management of the property (say following a divorce), it could be partitioned by a court and either interest sold. And when Bob gets that big court judgment against him, the creditor may wind up owning Bob's interest in the house.

• Joint Tenants with Right of Survivorship. If Bob and Susan decide to hold the property as joint tenants with right of survivorship (JTROS), again they'll each have an undivided interest. The chief difference is the "right of survivorship." That means if one dies, the property automatically belongs to the other, with no probate.

What if Bob and Susan own the house as joint tenants with a third person, say, Susan's mother, Ellen? When one owner dies, the other two automatically each own half (unless the deed or another agreement specifies otherwise). As in a tenancy in common, joint tenants are legally free to transfer their individual interests to someone else. Doing so ends the joint tenancy, so the new owner becomes a tenant in common with the remaining original owner(s). (The arrangement is complex if, say, Bob, Susan, and Ellen own the house as joint tenants and Ellen sells her interest to her friend Mary. Bob and Susan are still joint tenants with respect to two-thirds of the property, but tenants in common with respect to Mary's third.)

If Bob and Susan want to be joint tenants, they have to say so on the deed. The usual language for this is "Bob Smith and Susan Smith, as joint tenants with right of survivorship and not as tenants in common." That way, if there's a question, say from Susan's children from another marriage who think they should inherit her half interest in the property, the intent of the owners will be clear. If the deed doesn't specify joint tenancy, the law assumes that the owners are tenants in common (unless, in some states, if they're married to each other; see below).

SPLITTING UP

Chances are that very few couples are contemplating divorce when they buy themselves a home. But if they later agree to call it quits, what effect does the form of ownership indicated on the deed have on the property settlement?

Less than you'd think. To begin with, in about 90 percent of all divorces the property is divided up by the parties themselves out of court, often with the help of lawyers and mediators. They decide what's fair and reasonable in a process of give-and-take.

In contested divorces, it's up to the judge to decide who gets what. Years ago, courts in most states had no authority to redistribute property in a divorce, so their job was to sort out the legal titles. Only jointly held property was subject to judicial division. But these days, courts are more concerned with what's fair than with whose name is on a deed. They consider a wide range of factors, from the length of the marriage to the needs of each party.

So who gets the house? If there are minor children, usually the home goes to the custodial parent. If there are other assets to divide, the noncustodial parent may get a bigger share of them to balance out loss of the home. If not, courts typically award possession of the house to the custodial parent until the children grow up, when it's to be sold and the proceeds divided. If neither party can afford to maintain the home, the court may order it sold promptly and the equity split both ways.

Even if the property settlement specifies that the property is to be divided, it's critical to sign and record deeds to accomplish the conveyance and create a clear record of the title. Otherwise, sometime down the road you may have to track down a long-gone or uncooperative ex-spouse, or maybe file a quiet title lawsuit. That's a real mess. Get the deed.

If Bob or Susan want to be able to bequeath half of their house to someone else—say to Susan's children—they'd want to avoid joint tenancy. But if they each want their spouse to end up with the house, joint tenancy might be a good idea because then if one of them died, the house wouldn't be tied up in probate, which is the process of proving a will is valid and sharing out the property among heirs. In some states probate is a long and wearying process; in others it's very simple and no big deal.

• **Tenancy by the Entirety.** In Florida and a number of other states, usually in the East, married couples traditionally own property in a tenancy by the entirety. The form is rooted in the common-law concept that a husband and wife are one legal entity (that's one reason many states have eliminated the form, believing it's inconsistent with today's view of women). As with a joint tenancy, this form bears a right of survivorship, so if one spouse dies, the other automatically owns the property.

In most of the states that still recognize this form, a husband and wife who purchase property together are considered tenants by the entirety unless the deed specifically states that they are tenants in common (or joint tenants with right of survivorship) and not tenants by the entirety. Otherwise, a deed saying "to Bob Smith and Susan Smith, his wife," or "to Bob Smith and Susan Smith (husband and wife)," creates a tenancy by the entirety.

If Bob and Susan have reason to expect creditors to come after their house, they may want the protection offered by a tenancy by the entirety because property owned by both of them in that form generally isn't subject to a judgment against one owner (except in cases involving fraud), though this will vary by state. In the case of Bob's court judgment, the house would be safe because it belonged to the tenancy by the entirety, not just to Bob.

What if Susan decided she wanted to transfer her half of the house to her son by a former marriage? In Florida, like most of the states that recognize tenancy by the entirety, title can only be transferred if both spouses sign the deed indicating that both agree to the sale of their half interest. If they lived in Arkansas, New Jersey, New York or Oregon, either spouse could transfer his or her interest, including the right to survivorship.

• **Community Property.** Now suppose that Bob's company transfers him to California, where he and Susan buy a house in San Francisco. California is one of the nine states (the others are Arizona, Idaho, Louisiana, Nevada, New Mexico, Texas, Washington, and Wisconsin) that have adopted a different conception of the relationship of husband and wife, a conception rooted in Spanish and French law. In the absence of any directives to the contrary, these states consider all property acquired during a marriage, except by gift or inheritance, to be community property. Each spouse owns half of the community property. Community property means that there's no right of survivorship, so when one spouse dies half of the couple's property—including half of the house—goes through probate. To transfer the property to someone else, both husband and wife must sign.

Because California is a community property state, the law assumes that if Bob and Susan acquired their house during the marriage by the efforts of either spouse (not by inheritance or gift), the house is community property unless they specifically say otherwise in the deed. So if Bob's dear departed uncle Fred left the place to Bob in his will, it would be Bob's house should Bob and Susan split up. But if Bob and Susan make payments on the mortgage with his earnings or hers, it's community property. Why would a couple choose to hold a house as community property when they could choose to be tenants in common or joint tenants with right of survivorship?

Because there are two significant tax advantages in holding the house as community property rather than as a joint tenancy. One has to do with tax on capital gain, the difference between the selling price and the house's "basis," its cost when they got it. If the home is community property when Bob dies, it receives an entirely new tax basis when Susan inherits the whole. So if she sells it soon thereafter, there's no capital gain. But if they held it as joint tenants, only half an interest would change hands when Bob died, so only half the property would get a stepped-up basis. The capital gain upon sale is likely to cost Susan thousands of dollars in taxes.

The other tax advantage of community property involves estate taxes, and the fact that every American may bequeath up to $600,000 without paying estate taxes. If Bob and Susan held all their property as joint tenants, Susan would own it all when Bob died. He wouldn't transfer any property to her, because legally the property was already hers. Since he didn't transfer any property, his $600,000 lifetime exemption on estate taxes would in effect be lost. Since Susan's estate would increase by the value of his half of the house and all the other property held as joint tenants, her estate would be subject to hefty estate taxes when she died if the total value of her estate exceeded her $600,000 exemption.

Now suppose they'd opted for community property. As soon as he died, his share of the estate would be subject to estate taxes, but they'd be offset by the marital deduction. (No federal estate taxes are due on property bequeathed from one spouse to another, but special rules apply if the surviving spouse is not a U.S. citizen.) Then when Susan died, the taxable share of her estate would be much lower.

Like Bob and Susan, you have to look at your own circumstances and decide which form is best for you. Again, which of these options is available to you depends on the state you live in. Every state except Louisiana permits joint tenancy and tenancy in common. The nine community property states are listed on page 9 of this chapter. See your lawyer if you want to know if tenancy by the entirety is permitted in your state.

If after reviewing all this information you decide to change your form of ownership, the paperwork is fairly simple. Basically the appropriate parties sign a new deed and file it with the local recorder of deeds.

The consequences of using the wrong deed or the wrong wording are serious, though, because your intent might not be clear. Should there be uncertainty in the future, your spouse or heirs might have to go to court to sort it out. So consult an experienced property lawyer to make sure you consider all the aspects of your situation and get the job done right.

A straightforward change will probably have a nominal cost, more if you get a thorough review and consultation. Still, it's well worth the price if it helps you meet your long-term goals for home ownership.

LIFE, LIBERTY, AND PROPERTY

Now on to the rights of home owners and some restrictions you should know about.

Why is it so satisfying to spend that first night in your very own home? Because owning a home really means something. The right to own property is so deeply embedded in the American legal system that the Bill of Rights puts the right to property on the same level as the rights to life and liberty. It declares that no one may deprive someone of life, liberty, or property without due process of law, and the government may not take private property for public use without paying fairly for it. (See the section on "eminent domain" in chapter 3.) The English political philosopher John Locke, whose ideas underlie the U.S. Constitution, proclaimed that "government has no other end than the preservation of property."

In general, what you do with the home you own is up to you. It's yours to maintain or neglect, preserve or remodel, keep, sell or give away, and enjoy as you see fit. If someone damages your property, you have a legal right to compensation. (To obtain that compensation, though, you may have to sue.) In addition,

• You may rent or lease your home or part of your home (depending on zoning restrictions) to someone else. However, if there is a mortgage on your home you should review it to make certain it contains no restrictions on your ability to rent your home while the mortgage is in existence. The law protects your right to decide who you'll allow to live there, so long as you don't discriminate on the basis of race, sex, religion, or other protected categories. If you rent out your home you have a legal right to inspect the property periodically, protect your property from damage, and receive a reasonable rent, with an option to evict renters who fail to uphold their end of the bargain. (See box, "Planning to Rent It Out?")

• You may use, sell, or restrict the use of your property's natural resources, from stands of timber on the surface to minerals lying beneath. Note, though, that because surface and underground water, oil, and gas move about without regard to property lines, you don't necessarily have the right to pump out as much as you want from a well on your property. Removing these resources is subject to state and federal regulation. For instance, if there's a stream running through your land, in most states you can't dam it up completely so your downstream neighbors get no water. (In some western states, the property owners who are farthest upstream can take as much water as they wish.)

• You may place limitations on the use of your home long after you die. You could, for instance, bequeath your property to your children, provided that they not sell or transfer it to anyone other than your direct descendants. In many states a restrictive covenant like that expires at the end of the state's limit on perpetuities—typically twenty-one years after the death of the last heir alive when the covenant was made.

A woman in Elyria, Ohio, wanted to make sure that her

beloved home wouldn't turn into an office or boardinghouse like so many others in her changing neighborhood, so she provided in her will that after her death the house should be razed. The local historical society objected in court, noting the home's distinctive architecture. The court ruled that since the deceased woman's request wasn't contrary to public policy, it should be carried out—unless the historical society could find a way to ensure that the house would forever be maintained for the use and enjoyment of the public.

Restrictions

Although the rights our society affords to home owners are extensive, they aren't absolute. The people who live around you have rights, too, so the law places certain restrictions on the use of your property. If you're not mindful of zoning, building codes, easements, water rights, and local ordinances on noise, you could find yourself in trouble.

• **Zoning.** To avoid urban mishmash, municipalities often restrict business and industry to particular areas. Others are zoned residential, including apartment buildings, or zoned strictly for single-family homes. If your neighborhood is zoned residential, you won't have to worry about a pool hall or gas station going up next to your house. The down side is that you may not be able to do everything you might want to with your home.

A typical residential zoning law may not preclude you from starting a home-based business that won't alter the character of the neighborhood, such as freelance writing, telephone sales, or mail-order distribution. But if the home-based business you envision is going to require signs or frequent traffic from customers, better check with the local department of building and zoning.

If you wish to make a change to your property that would violate zoning restrictions, one option is to apply for a **variance**, which is essentially permission from the governing body to deviate from the zoning laws. The zoning department will give you a packet of materials explaining the steps to take, which may involve a public hearing, an appearance before the planning commission, and approval by the town council. You might have to show that the change you have in mind is required by a hardship caused by the shape, condition, or location of your property, and won't change the character of the neighborhood or decrease your neighbors' property values.

Another option, if your plans call for a major change, is to apply for a **zoning change**. If, say, you live just beyond the edge of an area zoned commercial and you want to turn your nineteenth-century mansion into a doctor's office, you might be able to convince the zoning authorities to extend the boundaries a bit. Again, you'd have to show that the change wouldn't bring down property values. Such a request may spark opposition from your neighbors, though.

• **Private Restrictions** may also affect what you may do with your property. Usually limited to relatively new housing developments, these covenants, conditions, or restrictions are designed to maintain quality control—so that after you've bought a top-quality home, no one may erect a shack on the lot next door and collect junk cars in the backyard. Usually drawn up by the developer, private covenants often specify such things as lot size, minimum square footage, and architectural design. They may preclude the presence of livestock, satellite dishes, boats and motor homes, certain types of fences, and unsightly activities such as auto repair.

These covenants "run with the land," which means they bind all future owners of the property unless a sizable majority of property owners in the affected development join in releasing them. Covenants may restrict your use of your land even if municipal zoning laws permit the proposed use. You should have received a copy of them from your real estate agent, attorney, or title insurance office when you bought your home. If not, they should be available from the homeowners' association (if there is one) or from the county recorder's office. As with zoning, you may be able to negotiate a minor variance, such as building an addition that's two feet taller than the covenant's limit.

Restrictive covenants may be enforced by a court of law if negotiations fail and a neighbor who objects to a violation files a lawsuit. The objecting party, however, must not have violated that restriction himself. And if your neighbor watched you reroof your house and waited until you were finished before complaining that the shingles were the wrong color, he probably won't get very far in court. Ditto if enough other people have violated the restriction to render it meaningless. (For more on these restrictions and on homeowners' associations, see chapter 2, "Sharing Ownership.")

• **Building Codes.** The local government is likewise concerned with maintaining quality, but its concerns have less to do with aesthetics and more to do with safety. Local building codes include specifications for such things as plumbing and wiring. If you're having home improvements made, you might need to get a building permit before you start and have the work inspected to make sure it complies with the codes. (See chapter 6, "Remodeling?")

• **Easements** grant someone else a right to use part of your property for a specific purpose, such as permitting a power company to run an electrical line over your backyard. They're recorded at the county courthouse and normally turn up in a title search. (See chapter 3 for more information.)

• **Historic Homes.** You might expect restrictions if your grand old home is listed on the National Register of Historic Places, but private owners are free to alter, add to, convert, or even (surely not!) demolish their home even if it's on the list. The only restriction is that no federally funded or federally licensed program may harm a home on the list without a hearing before a federal agency. Your restoration projects may be eligible, though, for a federal preservation grant on a 50 percent matching basis.

Check with your local landmark commission or historic preservation board to find out about relevant state or local restrictions.

• **Restricted Activities.** In general, what you do in the privacy of your home is your own business. Two exceptions: when your activities are illegal and/or when those activities make it difficult for other people to enjoy their own homes. If you mow your lawn at 4 A.M. or blast your stereo until your neighbors' windows rattle, don't be surprised if someone calls the police. Local noise ordinances may restrict the hours during which you can conduct certain noisy activities.

Most activities that are illegal in public are also illegal in private—such as selling cocaine or serving alcohol to minors. Police generally need a search warrant to enter your home, and to get one they must show "probable cause"—reasonable evidence that they're likely to find something illegal inside.

Respect these few restrictions and you'll find that home ownership provides you with a welcome retreat from the cares of the world.

CHAPTER TWO

■

Sharing Ownership

Condos, Co-ops, and Other Common-Interest Communities

"A MAN'S HOME IS HIS CASTLE." That means he can do whatever he wants with it, right? Well, maybe. If his castle is perched all alone on a hill, what he does with it is pretty much his own business. But what if his castle is rather small and shoehorned between dozens of others, with more people's castles stacked on top and below? That's when the lord of each particular castle may need to be subject to a list of restrictions, in the interest of keeping the whole community happy.

That's what some thirty-two million people in the United States have discovered, those who own or live in the country's 150,000 common-interest communities. Whether it's an exclusive brownstone cooperative in New York City, a high-rise beachfront condominium in Miami, or a cluster of townhouses in Des Moines, a common-interest community brings together people who share a certain vision of good living. These communities, most popular in areas where the cost of individual lots is prohibitive, are carefully designed to be attractive and relatively affordable. Many include amenities like tennis courts and swimming pools. And, unlike rental apartments, they allow residents to build equity in their own homes.

The idea is catching on fast. The nation's first condominium, the Greystoke, was built in Salt Lake City in 1962. Counting condominiums, cooperatives, and planned communities, common-interest communities encompassed 701,000 units by 1970. Five years later the number had jumped to 2,031,439. And by 1990, there were 11,638,921 units, housing one out of eight Americans.

The key to the success of these forms if also one of the biggest bugbears: strict restrictions on what owners can do with their property. The reason a spacious planned unit development is such an attractive place to live is that community regulations prohibit any given owner from painting his house purple or erecting a shed in the backyard. But those very restrictions also cause more tension and litigation than any other aspect of common-interest community living: whether Mrs. Taylor can keep her beloved Afghan hound or Mr. Smith can land his helicopter on the roof.

And because everyone is a part owner of the buildings and amenities common to all, when it's time to landscape the grounds or replace the windows, everyone has to pay. That aspect of community living causes nearly as much tension as the restrictions. For instance, a prestigious high-rise condo in Boston was in turmoil for months over whether to repair its leaky windows or replace them.

In theory, no one would buy into a common-interest community without examining its covenants and restrictions and agreeing to play by those rules. But in many cases a developer hoping to sell a unit makes promises that go against the community's restrictions—say, that it's perfectly fine to keep your potbellied pig. Or maybe you saw a reference in your deed to "covenants, conditions, and restrictions," but didn't know that the homeowners' association created by those documents decides whether or not you may put up a fence.

If you own a unit in one of these communities, it's important to understand the form of the community, what laws and regulations govern it, and how your community association operates.

WHAT'S YOUR TYPE?

Although the condominium has only been part of America's housing scene for some thirty years, the concept of shared ownership is much older. As early as the eleventh century, when many European towns were constricted by protective walls, German merchants devised a system for owning one floor of, say, a three-story residence. Belgium enacted the first true condominium statute in 1924, with other European and Latin American nations close behind. The condominium statute enacted in Puerto Rico in 1959 became the basis for early U.S. statutes, after a delegation of Puerto Rican businessmen convinced Congress to allow the Federal Housing Administration to insure mortgages secured by condominium units.

Meanwhile, a few residential neighborhoods were pioneering concepts of shared ownership of a private park. In 1831, developer Samuel Ruggles created a board of trustees to maintain Gramercy Park for the enjoyment of the owners of the surrounding homes. More than a century and a half later, the board still entrusts each home owner with keys to the park. In the past twenty-five years, consumer demand has spurred the burgeoning of common-interest communities nationwide. Creative developers have designed a wide assortment of variations on the theme, with a confusing array of names and forms of ownership.

Still, certain characteristics can be found in all common-interest communities. Unlike the haphazard growth of most residential areas, these communities are designed specifically for a certain type of community living by a single developer (or in the case of existing buildings, a single converter). They're created by a specific set of documents, usually drawn up by the developer and subject to change by the membership. And when the developer or converter bows out, the community's affairs are governed by an association of all unit owners through its elected board. The board has the authority to enforce the restrictions and collect assessments to pay for maintenance, operation, and improvements.

These mandatory assessments set common-interest communities apart from other housing developments, giving you both the advantages of pooled resources and the disadvantages of common control.

There are three basic types of common-interest communities with three distinct types of ownership: the cooperative, the condominium, and the planned community governed by a home-owners' association. You can't tell which is which by looking at the architectural form of the buildings—for example, in some states **site condominiums** look just like single-family detached

A BLOCK OF AIR?

*Owning real estate means owning land. Right? Not necessarily. Mid-rise and high-rise condominiums rely on the concept of the **air space block**. While the title to a single-family house or townhouse typically includes the land underneath it and the air above it, if you own a high-rise apartment there are other owners above and below. So you hold title, in effect, to a block of air—within four walls, a ceiling, and a floor.*

Within that air space block, your documents may allow you to alter or remove nonsupporting walls, replace the light fixtures, change the carpet however you wish, and make other changes that don't infringe on your neighbors' property rights. You're usually responsible for the maintenance and repair of paint, wallpaper, fixtures, and appliances, except for wires and pipes running through your walls that serve other units, too.

If you're accustomed to rental apartments, you might be surprised to learn that your condo building manager isn't responsible for fixing your hot water heater or air conditioner. Even the inside of the wall might belong to you, so if a maintenance crew punches a hole in the drywall to repair the pipes, it may well be your responsibility to repair the damage.

Who owns what can be a constant source of friction for condo owners. Before you storm down the hall to lodge a complaint, better check your documents to see whose problem it really is.

homes but the land, not the home, is part of the condominium—and the form of ownership has significant legal implications. Be sure you know what type yours is. (The form of ownership is specified in the community's **declaration**, essentially its constitution, which is found in the public record.)

The oldest—and now least common—form is the **cooperative**, found primarily in New York and Chicago. In a cooperative, you buy into a corporation or association that owns the entire building. You pay a monthly rent or "maintenance charge," which is a proportionate share of the association's cash requirements for mortgage payments, operation, maintenance, repair, taxes, and reserves. But you don't actually own any real estate—the cooperative association owns it all. And you are a tenant of the cooperative association, which is the landlord.

A **condominium** is essentially the opposite: you have exclusive title to the air space within your own unit, and you share ownership of the common elements (such as corridors, elevators, and tennis courts) with all the other unit owners as tenants in common (see chapter 1). You're free to mortgage your unit or sell it. As in a cooperative, all unit owners must pay their share of the assessment for operation, maintenance, repair, and reserves. The association is responsible for enforcing the rules and maintaining the common elements, but in most cases it doesn't actually own anything.

A **planned community**, a common-interest community that is neither a condominium nor a cooperative, usually takes one of two forms. The **planned unit development** (PUD) is a hybrid combining certain aspects of cooperatives and condominiums. In these communities, you the home owner hold title to a unit—in many cases, a single-family, detached house, often including the land underneath it and the air above it. But all common areas, such as parks and playgrounds, belong to the incorporated association, which all owners are required to join. The association is responsible for maintaining common areas and, in some cases, house exteriors. You pay a monthly, quarterly, or annual assessment for common-area expenses and reserves.

In another form, the **reciprocal easement community**, a common easement crosses the individually owned parcels, so that common driveways, party walls, and shopping centers are maintained jointly by the owners through assessments.

Note that the legal form of the community has nothing to do with its architectural design. For instance, a townhouse community—one with attached two-story houses—may be organized as a condominium, a planned community, or even a cooperative. An urban brownstone might be converted into a cooperative or a condominium. Because some states have stricter regulation of condominiums than of cooperatives and planned unit developments, developers in those states sometimes choose a legal form that you wouldn't expect from looking at the buildings. In Connecticut,

FEDERAL PROTECTION

Although most laws governing common-interest communities are created by individual states, federal law provides some protection for homeowners in these communities.

What protection do I have as a buyer?

The sale of units under development in a common-interest community of over twenty-five parcels is governed by the Interstate Land Sales Full Disclosure Act. This act requires the delivery of an offering plan and provides for a seven-day **rescission period**, which means that you can get out of the deal up to seven days later if you decide it's not for you.

The same act also sets standards for truth in advertising of communities.

May a condominium exclude families with children?

Not usually. Under the Fair Housing Act of 1988, common-interest communities may no longer discriminate against families with children unless they meet the act's strict qualifications for senior citizen communities. Otherwise, it's no longer legal to advertise a community as being for adults only, or to steer would-be buyers elsewhere because their children wouldn't be welcome.

If I'm disabled, does the community have to adapt its facilities to my abilities?

Yes. The Fair Housing Amendments Act requires community associations to permit construction of facilities for disabled residents, which they may be required to remove when they leave. Further, all new multifamily buildings must provide access for the handicapped in every unit that is on the ground floor or that is accessible by elevator. Under HUD regulations, this includes wide doors, free passage for wheelchairs through units, bathroom walls strong enough for grab bars, and access to at least a representative portion of the amenities. HUD estimates that the regulations will increase the cost of each unit by about $2,000.

IS YOUR ASSOCIATION ADEQUATELY INSURED?

Condominium associations typically carry several insurance policies to cover damage to building exteriors and common elements, plus liability for injuries on the premises. In addition, they usually carry directors' and officers' liability policies in case the board members are sued over their decisions, and an umbrella liability policy to cover catastrophic judgments. Unit owners pay their portions of the premiums as part of their regular assessments.

As a unit owner, you're responsible for homeowner's coverage on the contents of your unit, including paint and wallpaper and, perhaps, appliances and carpeting, as well as your own living expenses in the event of a fire or other casualty. This kind of coverage is similar to an apartment owner's policy. You have a right to see the association's master policy, which the association generally must supply within thirty days of your request. For a quicker response, ask the insurance company directly for a copy of the building policy. With that and a copy of the association's declaration in hand, your insurance agent can help you determine how much homeowner's insurance you need.

In a planned community, the declaration or bylaws will determine whether to insure the exteriors and common areas of the entire

for example, there are PUD townhouses, single-family detached cooperatives, and reciprocal-easement high rises.

GOVERNING LAWS

Imagine a crazy quilt, with snips and scraps of many-patterned fabric sewn together every which way. That's a fair image of the laws governing common-interest communities. While some federal laws have provisions aimed at condominiums, most of the substantive law—and confusion—lies in an ever-changing patchwork of state statutes. Then each individual community is governed by its own declaration and articles, a set of bylaws, and various regulations and decisions promulgated by the association board. Finally, given the extensive litigation over the *development under one blanket policy (with home owners responsible for the contents of their homes) or to have residents buy their own. Blanket policies are often less expensive than the sum of all the individual policies, and only one deductible applies if several homes are damaged by, say, a tornado. Collectively purchasing such a policy also eliminates the need for the association to verify that each owner maintains the coverage required by the documents.*

While you're looking at the master insurance policy, ask your agent if the association is adequately insured. Full replacement cost is important, as the victims of Hurricane Andrew learned recently. And if someone is seriously injured on the property and the association's liability policy doesn't cover the judgment, each unit owner could be assessed for a portion of the cost. Your homeowners' policy, if broad enough, should protect you against these and other emergency assessments resulting from a casualty or liability loss. Without your own coverage, however, you could be subject to a catastrophic assessment. If there's danger of flooding, the association should have a separate flood policy (see page 60).

Note that insurers almost never include coverage for damage caused by pollution, such as leaking underground tanks. Accordingly, association boards need to be very careful about assessing any potential risks and eliminating them before a problem occurs.

authority of particular associations, various courts have interpreted statutes, rules, and regulations, often based on common law (not statutory) principles developed over the centuries.

Condominium statutes vary considerably from state to state, and many lack protections for consumers. While some provide only the barest framework for creating a condominium, others are incredibly complex and detailed. Florida, where nearly three million people live in condominiums, understandably has the most extensive regulation of all—perhaps because of the number of retirees accustomed to an active life, who now put their energy into demanding legislative solutions to problems they face with their associations. In 1991, Florida's legislature passed 161 amendments to its condominium statute—including four separate laws regulating bingo.

(Several of these were changed again the following year—before they even became effective.)

Documents

Under normal circumstances, unit owners primarily need to be aware of the documents governing their own community. State laws require common-interest communities to prepare these documents and make them part of the public record.

If you want to know the basics about your community's land, buildings, and other improvements, the location of each unit, the common elements, and the intended use of each unit, take a look at the **declaration of condominium**, also called a **master deed**. The same document for a planned unit development is called in most states the **declaration of covenants and restrictions**, or sometimes just **restrictions**. This document has to do with the physical arrangement; under laws of many states, it need not contain much in the way of operational detail.

For an understanding of your community's legal setup and management structure, take a look at its **articles of incorporation** (these are called **articles of association** in nonincorporated associations). The articles include the power of the board to make, alter, and repeal reasonable bylaws.

The more detailed information you might need to know is most likely contained in the **bylaws**. Bylaws tell how the managing board will be elected and define its duties and powers. They tell whether the board will manage the property or engage a management firm. They contain ground rules critical to settling disputes that might arise, such as how assessments and reserves are to be determined and to what extent board decisions bind unit owners.

Although bylaws in most corporations may be altered freely by the board of directors or by a simple majority of the members, many condominium statutes require a two-thirds or even three-quarters majority to change the declaration or bylaws—which is often nearly impossible to achieve given the apathy of many unit owners. States that have adopted the Uniform Condominium Act allow a bit more flexibility, to allow communities to adapt to changing conditions. Wherever you live, though, get used to your community's bylaws, because they're almost certainly here to stay.

If you're concerned about details of community living, ask about additional **rules and regulations** your board might have established in the course of operating the community. These might specify how parking spaces are allocated, how big residents' dogs may be, and what color draperies are allowed to show through the windows. Generally the rules and regulations govern the common elements, while restrictions on the interior of the unit are found in the declaration.

If you believe that your board has overstepped its authority in a given regulation, it's possible to have a judge review it. For instance, a dissident board member in a Chicago condo complex sued his board in an effort to ensure fair elections. The board kept itself entrenched for years through a system of proxy voting that garnered votes from absentee ownership. In reviewing such cases, courts tend to consider four questions:

- Is the rule consistent with the declaration and other superior documents?
- Was the rule adopted in a good faith effort to serve a purpose of the community?
- Are the means adopted to serve the purpose reasonable?
- Is the rule consistent with public policy?

If a court rules that the answer to one of these questions is no, it might throw out the rule in question.

YOU AND THE ASSOCIATION

If you belong to the National Berry Pickers' Association, membership is voluntary and it's up to you whether to follow the directives of the leadership. Not so with the associations governing most common-interest communities. If you own one of the units, you're a member. And if the association within its powers adopts a rule, it has the legal authority to enforce it. A community association gains its authority from the legal documents that created it: the declaration, articles, and bylaws. State statutes often back up that authority, whether in the statutes governing nonprofit corporations, the specific condominium or common-interest community act, or both. Broadly speaking, a community association may hold property, sue and be sued, receive gifts and bequests, make charitable contributions, make contracts, borrow or invest money, and assess unit owners for their share of the expense of maintaining and operating the community. Some state statutes grant even more far-reaching powers.

The board of directors is elected by the membership to carry out day-to-day operations and oversee enforcement of the rules and restrictions. A typical board has five to seven members elected on a rotating basis and a set of officers.

It's up to the association board to enforce the rules and restrictions when a unit owner ignores them. One way is by levying fines against the owner. If the owner refuses to pay, the board may file a lien against the property and, if necessary, foreclose on it to get the money. Another approach is for the association to sue the violator, seeking an injunctive order to stop the practice in question. A violator who refuses to follow the court order could be in contempt of court.

In theory, any unit owner may sign a complaint against a neighbor to initiate a mini-court process that could lead to fines. In practice, though, most unit owners are hesitant to sign formal complaints against people next door, even though they voice their concerns loudly to the board. If the community hires a management company—standard practice in larger communities—the company's routine maintenance inspections include checking for violations of the restrictions. The employee who discovers the infraction then serves as a complaining witness to the board, which more than likely will initially send someone to talk to the violator. Most board members try to be evenhanded in their enforcement, as they don't want to be criticized for nailing one violator and winking at another.

If the board decides to resort to the courts, it must do so promptly or risk losing the authority to enforce the restriction. If the restrictions say you can't build a toolshed and you do anyway, board members can't walk past it every day for a year and then sue to have you remove it.

Although association disputes do land in court—more often than you might suppose—board members spend most of their time dealing with much more mundane matters. Mrs. Bennett keeps parking in Mrs. Anderson's space. Mr. Bates insists on storing an old refrigerator on his balcony. Ms. Brattleboro is furious about the new special assessment.

Serving on a board is often a difficult, thankless job, and when one member resigns it may be hard to find a suitable replacement. Some associations are debating the advisability of allowing associations to pay people for serving on the board. Very few states prohibit it.

One of the most thankless tasks of the association board is also one of the most important: assessing owners for the kinds of improvements, maintenance, and services that keep up their property values. When the board raises the monthly assessment or votes for a special assessment, expect fur to fly. Members may share walls and walkways but they rarely share a common view of just what projects need to be done and how much they should cost. Some plan to stay a long time and want long-term solutions; others have plans to move on soon and don't want changes that cost more money than they're worth in the short run. And some simply can't afford to pay a sharply increased monthly assessment.

In a few states, associations may not raise the assessment more than a set amount without approval from the membership. In Illinois, for example, condominium boards must hold a referendum of unit owners if their budget increase is more than 15 percent. And many condominium declarations adopted ten or fifteen years ago set similar dollar caps on assessment without owner approval. Some declarations require approval for assessments for improvements costing more than a certain amount, but not for maintenance expenses no matter how large.

Some state statutes and declarations mandate certain levels of reserves, to guard the community's financial stability and prepare for inevitable capital expenditures. Even without a mandate, a board is wise to build up an adequate reserve to avoid

OWNING WITH A FRIEND

Whether it's two lovers setting up housekeeping, three singles look-ing for affordable housing, or four couples buying a vacation cabin, an increasing number of unmarried people are sharing ownership of a house, condo unit, or recreational housing. Developers court-ing the "mingles" market are even building houses with two master bedroom suites.

However appealing in theory, owning a home with someone you're not married to can bring special problems. People who enter the arrangement primarily for financial reasons may not share the same goals for use of the property, which can lead to even more tension than between people with an emotional commitment to each other. And when unmarried home owners decide to split up, there's no divorce court with an established body of law to help protect everyone's rights.

If you're thinking of sharing ownership with a friend or relative, make sure your goals are compatible before you buy. If you've agreed to split maintenance costs, does that include landscaping, remodeling, or rehabbing? Do you both want to make—and pay for—the same changes? How do you each feel about entertaining? How much time do you want to spend together? If the property will be a vacation home, how will you decide who gets it when? What standards of cleanliness do you expect?

Then draw up a co-ownership agreement that lays the ground rules and answers these questions:

having to require a massive special assessment when, say, the furnace gives out.

When unit owners are doing well, they may grouse about the assessment but chances are they'll pay it. But what if a unit owner is in serious financial trouble, with several thousand dol-lars' worth of assessments unpaid? If the owner goes bankrupt, the creditors line up for their share of what's left—and the com-munity association is normally far down the line, well behind the bank that holds the mortgage. But if the association can't

- *Will the partners' monthly mortgage payments be equal or based on each person's income?*

- *If you decide on unequal contributions, how will you divide the profits when you sell the home?*

- *Splitting maintenance costs fifty-fifty makes sense, but what if it's a duplex and only one owner puts in new carpeting? Consider using a condominium as a model, so the partners each bear the cost of improvements to their own units, but divide the cost of improvements to common elements such as roofs, exterior walls, and landscaping.*

- *If one partner decides to leave, does the other have the right to buy his interest? How will the value be determined? Specify in the agreement how an appraiser will be chosen.*

- *If one partner moves out without selling, should there be a penalty (in the form of a lien on the partner's interest) for not making mortgage payments?*

- *In the case of a duplex, if one partner moves out, do rental tenants have to be approved by both owners? Who bears the cost of tenant damage or eviction?*

Hire an attorney to help you negotiate and draw up this contract. A couple hundred dollars spent now can save you major headaches later.

obtain the bankrupt owner's assessment, all the other property owners in the community have to cover it.

One provision of the Uniform Common Interest Ownership Act, in effect in Pennsylvania, West Virginia, Connecticut, Alaska, and several other states, is to give community associations a "super-priority lien," putting them first in line for the bankrupt unit owner's share of the past six-months' assessments. Numerous states are considering this provision, with, as might be imagined, considerable opposition from the banking lobby.

COPING WITH PROBLEMS

As you might expect whenever people live side by side, problems do arise. Here are a few of the most common, with some suggestions for dealing with them.

• **If you want a variance.** Under the rules of most community associations, you can't make changes to the exterior of your home without the consent of the board. Often the board delegates the review of plans to an architectural control committee that sets standards and uses them to rule on whether you can add a skylight or put on a screen door. As a home owner, you submit your plans to the committee and cross your fingers. Be aware, though, that courts have found that covenant committees do not have the authority to approve major violations of the restrictive covenants.

As with zoning requests in most municipalities, the governing documents in some common-interest communities state that if you haven't heard from the board within thirty days of your request, consider it approved. In that case, most courts would uphold your right to go ahead with the plan. It's a rarity, though, for boards to let their decisions be made by default.

If the board says no, you'll either have to change your plans or steel yourself for a major battle. One New Jersey home owner sued his association in 1982 after its board denied him permission to build a deck. The case was in and out of court for years, with neither side willing to budge.

• **If you have a dispute with a neighbor.** What if your neighbors practice the trumpet at 5 A.M., their children race tricycles in the hall, or they insist on parking in your assigned space? Step one is to check the restrictions and regulations governing the association to see whether the practice in question is a violation. Then talk about it, first to the neighbor in question and then to someone on the board. In many cases board members act as mediators to help unit owners work things out informally. If one party is clearly violating the restrictions, the board may ask you to sign a formal complaint to begin a proceeding that could lead to fines against your neighbor or even a court injunction to stop the behavior.

If the problem isn't addressed in the documents and a polite request doesn't help, one option is to try alternative dispute resolution. Mediation brings in someone trained in helping people work out their own solutions, while arbitration submits the case to an arbitrator for a decision, which may or may not be legally binding. Either approach is likely to be quicker, less expensive, and less stressful than going to court.

Again, it's important to act promptly if a neighbor's behavior makes your life unpleasant. If you've put up with the offensive behavior without comment for ten years, you may have trouble proving your point.

• **If your community has too many rental tenants.** Condominiums can be an excellent tax shelter for a small-time investor, who might buy a unit in a vacation area, occupy it two weeks a year, and have a management company rent it out week by week the rest of the year. In other cases a developer who hasn't been able to sell all the units will cover expenses by renting them out like apartments.

Owner-occupants often object to renters, who are perceived as not caring about the property enough to maintain it properly. Likewise, absentee owners generally want to keep up the rental value, but don't want to pay for extras. And although restrictions apply to tenants as well as to owner-occupants, they're more difficult to enforce. (But if the board slaps a lien on a unit owner because of the tenant's behavior, the owner may well terminate the tenant's lease.)

If a majority of the unit owners believe the number of renters is a problem, they may be able to band together and convince the board to call for a vote on a change to the restrictions that would limit leases.

• **If your converter defaults.** Although cooperative ownership is rare in most parts of the country, it's a primary form of home ownership in New York City. Over the past few years, a glut of cooperative conversions in New York and some changes in the laws governing them have put some conversion sponsors in deep financial trouble.

When the owner of an apartment building decides to convert it to a cooperative, the building's residents have a legal right to remain as rent-controlled tenants for as long as they wish, unless 50 percent of them decide to buy. Typically quite a few choose that option. That means there's a hybrid phase during the conversion process, in which some apartments are owned by their residents while the rest still belong to the conversion sponsor. Until the rent-controlled tenants move out or choose to buy, the sponsor is responsible for more in monthly maintenance fees than he receives in rent. Many sponsors have defaulted, whether by not paying maintenance on unsold shares, not paying the mortgage, or both. The entire corporation then faces foreclosure or bankruptcy.

If that happens to your cooperative, there are several ways to avoid disaster. If the sponsor has financed the unsold shares, the sponsor's lender would do well to begin paying maintenance on those apartments as quickly as possible to protect the value of the collateral, then try to sell the shares to the tenants or pay them to move and resell the units. If not, the shareholders need to take control of the board of directors, terminate the sponsor's proprietary lease, and cancel his stock. Then the rent goes to the corporation. Quick action is critical to keep the building from deteriorating in the meantime.

• **If problems arise with the developer.** In an increasing number of cases, condominium associations have sued their developers over shoddy construction, breach of contract, negligence, or fraud. These lawsuits are complex, time-consuming, and expensive, often involving hundreds of people and millions of dollars. But the law expects a developer who cuts corners on construction or breaks promises to the unit owners to make up for the damage.

If the problem involves only your unit, it's up to you to engage an attorney and try to settle the matter out of court, if possible. But if it involves common areas or common funds, the association may assess all unit owners to pay its legal fees in pursuing the developer. In some cases the developer may agree to arbitration, to save the time and expense of a lawsuit. The important thing, though, is to act quickly, because statutes of limitations can prohibit lawsuits filed as little as a year after sale. And the longer you wait, the harder it is to find witnesses or collect a judgment.

• If the board doesn't do its job. The people who are best qualified to serve on association boards are often too busy to do so. That leaves people who are well-meaning but inexperienced, and those with too much time on their hands. But these people are charged with the management of a large community and a considerable amount of money. Some boards neglect the enforcement of rules or misuse the funds entrusted to them.

If you suspect financial problems, you're entitled to review the association's financial documents, including its budget, financial report, bank loan documents, and record of reserves. Together with other concerned unit owners, you may hire an independent accountant for an audit even if the board refuses to do so.

If you believe the board has become autocratic and tyrannical, review the minutes of the board meetings to see whether decisions were made in accordance with the association's bylaws, rules, and regulations. Was there proper notice of meetings? Were all procedures proper? If not, some of the board's actions may be void.

When the board has seriously mismanaged its responsibilities, you have two basic options. One is to file a lawsuit against the board for breaching its duties. Be aware, though, that the board has a right to assess the unit owners to pay for its own defense, so you'll be paying for both sides. Arbitration or mediation may be a less costly approach, if your bylaws permit them. The other option is to run for a position on the board yourself and convince some well-qualified neighbors to do the same. In the long run, that's probably a better solution.

The key to smooth operation of a common-interest community is communication—especially between the board and the rest of the association. People are less likely to object to rules if they have advance notice and believe they've had their say.

CHAPTER THREE

■

Defending Your Title

What Title Insurance Will Do for You—and What It Won't

A FTER AN HOUR in the lawyer's conference room, you've signed your name in half a dozen places and written checks for the down payment and fees. Standing up and stretching, you shake hands with the lawyer, the banker, and the sellers. Despite all your worries, the closing has gone smoothly and you're free to gather up your papers, thank everyone, and head down the hall. Then you step outside and it hits you that you now officially own that wonderful home.

You can't help peeking again at the paper with WARRANTY DEED written in bold letters at the top. Everything looks fine: the lengthy legal description, the sellers' signatures, the statement in lofty language that you are the owner in fee simple, to have and to hold said premises forever. The document is authoritative, traditional, and reassuring. So why did your lender insist on title insurance?

Because residential property often has a long and convoluted history of previous owners and transactions. You can't tell by looking at the property and the current deed whether the title is good, as if it were a grapefruit in the supermarket. For all you know, the people you bought the house from might have slipped out and gotten a second mortgage on the property two days before closing, or neglected to pay a $5,000 special assessment for the new sewer. Perhaps the swimming pool is located right on the electric company's easement for underground lines. Maybe the prior owner decided not to tell you that her ex-husband has a

lien—a claim on the property for repayment of debt—on the house for half the proceeds of the sale.

Title insurance is like a stockade fence around your property, protecting it from pirates who might creep out of the past. Chances are you'll never file a claim, but you'll be mighty glad to have title insurance if you do.

To a great extent, securing title insurance is an exercise in preventive law. Just as health insurance companies refuse to insure people with a history of medical problems, title insurance companies refuse to insure properties with a history of legal uncertainties. Accordingly, the title examiner combs the records with an expert eye and identifies any potential problems, such as an unpaid tax assessment or a neighbor's easement for right-of-way. The examiner then issues a preliminary report called a **commitment**, which lists these defects and informs you of any problems that the seller must correct prior to closing. If the company isn't willing to cover a particular matter and the seller can't or won't correct it, you can choose either to live with the problem or to bow out of the deal. If a title insurer refuses to write the policy at all, you can bet that the seller can't give you good title.

But even a stout stockade fence can't protect you from bolts out of the blue. Title insurance policies clearly state that they don't cover matters that arise after the effective date of the policy. So if a court files a judgment against you two months after closing, secured by a lien on your house, that's not the title company's problem. Nor is the city's decision to condemn your property to build a new fire station. And because title companies refuse to insure risks they discover in their search, the insurance policy covers only surprises: hidden problems caused before the effective date of the policy but only coming to light later.

That's why it's important to know not only what your title insurance will cover, but also what it won't: what scenarios might arise in the future that would challenge your title to the property. This chapter offers an introduction to titles, title insurance, and various encumbrances that could endanger your ability to enjoy your home.

TITLE INSURANCE OPTIONS

Refinancing your mortgage? Buying a second home? Unless you and your lender are content with an abstract, you'll need to buy title insurance. You have more than one option on where to get it.

If you employ a commercial title company to research your title, you won't necessarily be dealing with a lawyer. Some commercial title companies issue policies through lawyers, but others employ nonlawyer agents. Commercial title policies have some advantages. For example, if the holder of a title insurance policy relocates to another state and a title problem arises with the property in his former state, he may have the convenience of being able to deal with a branch office in his new locale if his policy was issued by a national commercial insurer. If his policy was issued by a state-bar-related insurer in the former state, however, there will be no branch office. There may also be some comfort to the insured to know that the liquidity of a national title insurer may not be affected as much as that of a state-bar-related title insurer in an area where there is a high claim rate as a result of an economic downturn. The national insurer's risk is spread across the country.

On the other hand, if you want to make sure your title is researched by a lawyer familiar with the complexities of real estate law, consider dealing with a bar-related title insurer, if one is available in your state. Such an insurer is essentially a real estate lawyer who sells title insurance.

The insurance policy, which is backed by an attorney's title guarantee fund, is no better or worse than those issued by for-profit companies. It even uses the same standard forms. The chief advantage is having the same person research the title and offer legal counsel.

For the names of attorneys in your area who offer bar-related title insurance, contact the National Association of Bar-Related Title Insurers, 1030 West Higgins Road, Suite 230, Park Ridge, Illinois, 60068; 708-698-0500.

EVIDENCE OF TITLE

Let's begin with the concept of **good title**. If you have good title to your property, you legally own it; whoever you bought it from owned it fair and square and had a right to sell it to you. Suppose that person bought it two years before from a con artist who knew it really belonged to someone out-of-state but forged a convincing deed. In that case, you couldn't obtain good title from that seller no matter how much you paid, because it wouldn't be his to sell. But with good title, you're legally free to buy the property, own it as long as you wish, and sell it to someone else.

A real estate title consists not only of ownership but also of a bundle of interests and rights to use the property, including minerals, crops, fixtures, water, and air space. (It also includes any toxic wastes that might be on the property, which might become the new owner's problem. See the section on toxic wastes in chapter 4.) The title search is designed to ensure that the entire bundle is tied together correctly and completely—or at least to determine which rights aren't included.

For instance, the fact that the prior owner legally owned the property doesn't help much if there's a major lien on the property. Unless the lien is paid off, the creditor could require the property to be sold to satisfy the debt. Liens and other claims that people or governments have on a property are called **encumbrances**. Broadly speaking, they diminish the value of the property or limit its use.

To ensure good title reasonably free of encumbrances, someone has to research the history of transactions involving the property. Historically this began with an **abstract** prepared by an attorney or an abstract firm, which included copies of all documents that recorded transactions involving the property. The buyer's attorney would examine the abstract and write a letter expressing the opinion that the seller did indeed have good title, subject to whatever encumbrances had surfaced in the process.

Especially in rural areas, some buyers still rely on abstract and opinion for evidence of title. People who love the land feel a certain affinity with abstracts, yellowed with time and replete with the names of Indians, French explorers, and early settlers. For many small-town lenders who know their area and much of its history, an abstract backed by the opinion of a local attorney is good enough. But metropolitan mortgage lenders, who rarely know much about any given property, have made abstracts and opinions obsolete by insisting on title insurance.

The chief problem with abstracts is their lack of accountability. What happens if the abstract company or the lawyer issuing an opinion on the property fails to uncover a flaw in the title that costs you, the new owner, a great deal of money? You could sue, but you'd have to prove that someone was negligent. With title insurance, the insurer agrees to pay covered claims whether anyone was negligent or not. Like abstract and opinion, title insurance results from a thorough investigation of the public record, but it is backed by insurance.

How Title Insurance Works

In a way, title insurance is the opposite of your home's casualty and liability insurance, which repays you in case of injury or damage occurring after the effective date of the policy. Title insurance covers only matters that occurred before the policy's effective date, but were discovered later. Instead of having to pay premiums year after year to maintain coverage, you have to pay only once, though you would probably have to buy another title insurance policy on the property should you refinance. Many lenders insist on a new policy before refinancing, to make sure their new loans will have first priority. They want to know if you've taken out a second mortgage, gotten a home improvement loan, or been subject to a court judgment between the original mortgage and this one.

That brings us to the two kinds of title insurance policies. When you bought your home, perhaps the seller bought an owner's policy for you, or perhaps you bought the owner's policy. That practice varies, depending on what part of the country you're in. Either way, though, probably you had to buy a "mortgagee" policy for your lender. The **owner's policy** covers losses or damages you suffer if the property really belongs to someone else, if there's a defect or encumbrance on the title, if the title is unmarketable, or if there's no access to the land (say, if the person who owns the private road you'd have to use to your property refuses to grant permission to use it).

Your policy should have a section setting forth what is covered as of the effective date: ownership is free from defects or encumbrances (except for those listed in the policy); there is access to the land; you have the legal right to sell the property and convey good title (your title is marketable).

The lender's **mortgagee policy** protects the lender. It includes all four of the protections listed above, since lenders care about encumbrances too. Important clauses for the lender are those covering losses the lender would suffer if another creditor were first in line. Suppose you took out a $40,000 second mortgage and managed to keep that fact hidden while arranging refinancing for your first mortgage. Then suppose the second mortgage lender foreclosed and claimed a big chunk of the proceeds. The lender who refinanced your first mortgage would be able to recover the difference from the title company.

Owner's policies are more expensive, in part because the owner has a greater stake in the title. (The mortgage may be well under the value of the property). Accordingly the owner's policy is considered primary. If the same insurer issues both, the concurrent mortgagee policy will probably cost about a third as much. In part that's because the insurer doesn't have to search the records twice. More important, it's because a concurrent policy doesn't really increase the risk. Suppose the owner's policy is for $100,000, the mortgagee policy is $80,000, and the title turns out to be no good. The insurer reimburses the owners for their lost equity, say $20,000, and the lender for the value of the mortgage, say $80,000. With $100,000, the insurer has covered both policies.

The limits of the owner's policy is typically the market value of the house at the time of the purchase, while the mortgagee policy is for the amount of the mortgage. The premium is based on the amount of coverage, and the cost ranges widely, depending on location.

If you're refinancing, your new title insurer will probably rely on the work of the individual or company who did a title search when you bought the home, bringing it up to date. In that case, a search would be conducted from the date you purchased your home up to the date you are refinancing. However, this is only true if you provide a prior policy as evidence of good title. Then, if a big problem surfaces that the original title insurer should have caught, the second insurer may go after the first to cover the claim. Make sure to contact an attorney if you have questions about your title policy.

If you have an abstract and opinion, the insurer may bring it up to date and base the policy on that.

What's Not Covered

Title insurance policies are standard in most states, although the forms may vary somewhat from state to state. Owner's policies usually do not cover one or more of the following matters, often referred to as **standard exceptions**, unless, in most (but not all) states, an additional premium is paid and/or extra investigation or a survey is done and the necessary information is furnished to the title company. When the evidence is furnished and the additional insurance coverage is given, this is frequently referred to as "extended coverage." The standard exceptions are:

- claims of people who turn out to be living in the house (such as the prior owner's tenants or someone living without your knowledge in your lake cabin) if their being there isn't a matter of public record,
- boundary line disputes,
- easements or claims of easements not shown by public records,
- unrecorded mechanic's liens (claims against the property by unpaid home improvement contractors),
- taxes or special assessments left off the public record.

In addition, in much of the country (primarily the western states), mineral and/or water rights are a standard exception.

Other important exceptions from coverage include zoning, environmental protection laws, matters arising after the effective date of the policy, and matters created, suffered, or assumed by the insured. Other exceptions are subdivision and building codes, and matters known to the insured, not shown on the public records, and not disclosed to the insurer. Check your current policy to see what's on the list in case there's anything you should be concerned about. Exceptions need to be removed by special endorsements and probably will result in additional premiums.

COPING WITH CLOUDS ON YOUR TITLE

Liens

A **lien** is a claim to property for the satisfaction of a debt. If you refuse to pay a debt, whoever files the lien may ask a court to raise the money by foreclosing on your property and selling it, leaving you with the difference between the selling price and the amount of the lien. (Your mortgage lender, though, would probably be first in line for payment.) It's possible to lose a $200,000 house over a $5,000 lien—but not likely, because any home owner with the wherewithal to own such a house would almost surely not let it go over that.

There are several types of liens, any of which functions as a cloud on your title. If not removed, any of these liens can lead to foreclosure or inhibit your ability to sell your home.

- **Mechanic's lien (also called a "construction lien").** If contractors or subcontractors have worked on the house (or suppliers have delivered materials) but have not been paid, the law allows them to file a mechanic's lien against the property at the local recording office. These people are entitled to payment, and they have a right to foreclose on the property to obtain it.

  In some states contractors and subcontractors have to notify the home owner if they intend to file a lien, but in others your first word is notice of actual filing. If the prior owner had work done shortly before selling but neglected to pay the bill, the lien could come as a surprise to you—and unless you have extended coverage, your title insurance won't cover it.

  If you're the one who had the work done, you could still face a mechanic's lien if your contractor failed to pay your subcontractor or materials supplier. That's why you're well advised to withhold final payment until the contractor gives you a release-of-lien form signed by all subcontractors and material suppliers. (See chapter 6, "Remodeling?," pages 105–107.)

- **Divorce decrees.** If two home owners get divorced, chances are that the court will grant one of them the right to keep living in the house. When that owner sells it, though, the ex-spouse may be entitled to half the equity. The divorce decree would probably grant that spouse a lien on the property for that amount. If everything goes as it should, the closing will involve payment in full of each ex-spouse's share.

But things don't always go as they should. Suppose the ex-husband of the woman you bought the house from was subject to such a decree, but he had given her a **quitclaim deed** to the property conveying ownership to her but not mentioning his lien. She might leave town with both halves of the equity—and under some circumstances the lien would stay with the property. The ex might still have a right to extract his equity from it.

In that case the title insurer might disclaim responsibility because the lien isn't filed in the land records. However, in some jurisdictions the courts have ruled that insurers can't do that; when there's been a divorce, insurers are on notice that this problem could arise so they should check the divorce decree.

Likewise, if you bought a home with your spouse but later got divorced, your own divorce decree might give your ex a lien on the home for half the proceeds. That lien can hinder your ability to sell the home if your ex refuses to release it. A careful divorce lawyer will build a release mechanism—such as an escrow containing a deed and release—into the divorce decree.

- **Community association liens.** If you purchased your home in a common-interest community (such as a condominium, cooperative, planned unit development, or homeowner's association), the association might well have a lien for unpaid assessments. At the closing, often the title company or lender will receive a certificate of payment from the association to assure that this is not the case.

- **Unpaid child support.** Some states slap a lien on the property of divorced parents who fail to pay child support. That lien would have to be paid off before the property could be sold. In many cases the lien is tied to each child-support payment, so the property can be sold if the parent is current in his or her payments.

- **Court judgments.** A home owner who gets into financial trouble might wind up with a court order to pay a given debt, secured by a lien on his property. Again, the debt would have to be paid and the lien removed before the property could be sold.

If you discover a lien on your property, see your lawyer immediately to determine your best course of action. If the lien is valid and the amount in question is relatively small, an attorney might advise you to pay it off yourself to clear the title and avoid foreclosure. However, just paying it off is not enough. Have the payee sign a release-of-lien form, and file it at the county recording (or "land title") office to clear the title. You can then decide how to pursue whoever's responsible. (Be aware, though, that if you voluntarily pay an invalid lien, you will not be able to recover from the debtor.)

If the amount of the lien is major and you believe it's not your debt, consult with your attorney about what to do.

Taxes and Special Assessments

Usually the title search will turn up any unpaid property taxes, including those for the current year, and list them as exceptions in its title commitment. Then whoever conducts the closing will make sure the seller pays a *pro rata* share of the taxes due or gives the buyer a credit for the unpaid taxes.

If the public record doesn't show that back taxes are due, perhaps because of some clerical error, the title company may point to the standard exceptions and refuse to pay. In that case, it's up to the current owner to pay the taxes to avoid a lien on the property. If you have an "extended coverage policy," though, the insurer would have to pay the taxes and then seek recovery from the prior owner.

Likewise, if the city upgrades the sewer or puts in a new sidewalk, all affected home owners may be required to pay their proportionate share of the cost. Normally this is done through a special assessment voted by the city council and communicated to home owners with a notice. If your home's prior owner failed to pay it, it's your responsibility to do so because otherwise the city may foreclose on your property to extract payment.

An unpaid assessment will not always turn up in your title company's search. Although a record of the vote would be in the council's minutes, it wouldn't be in the public land record—so title companies routinely disclaim responsibility unless the insured has obtained extended coverage. It's often two or three years between the time the owner fails to pay a special assessment and the time the city files a lien against the property—in which case you, the new owner, may get a sudden unpleasant surprise.

If you get notice that the city or county has filed a lien against your property for unpaid taxes or special assessments, see your attorney to determine if the lien is valid. You may be advised to pay off the debt, then, depending on the amount, sue whomever sold you the house without paying the assessment. It's important to clear your title.

If you're the one who pays the debt, have the clerk draw up and sign a release-of-lien form. Then stop by the county recording office to file the form.

Easements

If there's an **easement** on your property, someone else may have a right to use part of it for a specific purpose. For instance, your beachfront property might have an easement granting public access to the waterfront. These are normally established by the developer at the time the subdivision is platted (mapped), to provide needed services to the development.

If a utility wants an easement that won't benefit a given property, such as using a strip of land for a high-voltage power line, it must pay the property owner for the property's diminished value (if the property owner refuses to grant the easement, the utility owner may exercise its power of eminent domain to force a deal; see below).

It's also possible for your neighbors to have an easement on your property, whether to use your driveway to get to their house or to restrict you from blocking their view of the lake. Or they might have a **profit** (short for the French term *profit a prendre*, which means "profit to be taken"), allowing them to remove something from your property such as raspberries, coal, or timber.

An easement or profit may be created by a deed, by a will, or by implication—say, if a previous owner divided a single lot in half and the only access to the back lot is through the front one. If a neighbor has been using your property in some way for a long time, say by maintaining his fence on a strip of your property, he may be able to secure a **prescriptive easement** to continue doing so whether you want him to or not. The mechanism to settle such a dispute is called a **quiet title** lawsuit.

Courts are willing to grant prescriptive easements when the neighbor has been engaging in the activity in question for a given number of years and the property owner hasn't physically stopped him, say by erecting a locked gate. Oddly, one of the requirements for gaining a prescriptive easement is the property owner's objections—such as your telling him not to drive on your road over and over for a period of years (that varies by state) but not keeping the gate closed. The reasoning seems to be that if you give me permission to do something, I can't claim it as a right.

Easements on your property are recorded at the county courthouse, but they may be scattered throughout the county building among various plats, deed books, and mortgage books. They generally turn up in a title search. Like encroachments (see below), they are often brought to light by a survey. If you don't have a survey done yourself, at least look at the owner's or lender's survey before the closing.

If you discover an easement, check the wording. When a document grants an easement to a particular person, the restriction usually terminates when he dies or sells the property. But if it's granted to someone for a term of years or to someone and "his heirs and assigns," it's probably in effect no matter who owns the property.

Unless and until the easement expires, your legal obligation is to refrain from interfering with that right. Again, unless you have extended coverage on your title insurance, your insurer isn't responsible for any loss you suffer because of an easement that wasn't recorded in the public record. At any rate, easements involve use of the property rather than ownership; if you're careful to respect them, they shouldn't cause problems.

Adverse Possession

Although you have a right to keep trespassers off your land, it's possible under the law for a trespasser who uses the property as you would yourself to actually become the owner. This entitlement is called **adverse possession**. It's unlikely to occur in an urban or suburban area, where lots are relatively small and home owners know when someone else has been using their property. But if you own a remote hunting cabin, you might not know that someone's been living there full time for years.

Adverse possession is similar to a prescriptive easement, where a court declares that, say, your neighbor has a right to keep his hedge on that strip of your land because it's been there for forty years. The difference is that while prescriptive easements concern use of the land, adverse possession concerns actual ownership.

In order for a claim of adverse possession to succeed, the trespasser has to show that his occupation of your property was open and hostile, which means without permission. As with prescriptive easements, granting the person permission to use the property cancels his claim to ownership by adverse possession.

His occupation must also have continued for a certain number of years, depending on the state. Generally it's ten to twenty or even thirty years, but sometimes less. And in many states, the trespasser must have paid local property taxes on the land.

This last requirement provides a way to ward off loss of a property through adverse possession. If you suspect that someone's been living in your hunting cabin, check the property tax records for that county to see whether anyone has made tax payments on it.

A bit of vigilance will prevent problems in this area. Post NO TRESPASSING signs to warn people that this is private land. Erect gates at entry points and keep them locked. Ask trespassers to leave, and call the police if they refuse.

If you suspect that someone in particular will keep on using your property (such as for a road or to obtain lake access) despite your efforts, consider granting written permission to keep on doing so, especially if the use does not interfere with your use. That way the party can never claim a right to your land. To make the arrangement clear, ask for a written acknowledgment, and, if reasonable, a payment.

Encroachments

When your neighbor's house, garage, swimming pool, or other permanent fixture stands partially on your property or hangs over it, that's an **encroachment**. So is your new addition if it starts twenty-three feet back from the sidewalk, when the local setback ordinance requires twenty-five feet.

It's even possible to encroach on an easement, for instance by locating the apron of your swimming pool on the telephone company's easement across your property for underground cables. In that case, the company would have a right to dig up the concrete and charge you for it.

In the case of the setback requirement, the neighbors could band together and sue you, hoping to get you to move the offending wall. Or you might have to live with your neighbors' disapproval, perhaps after paying a fine to the city for the violation.

In the case of a neighbor's roof overhanging your property or his fence being two feet on your side of the line, you may or may not be able to demand its removal. Your rights might depend on how obvious the encroachment is, and how long it has been in place. If it was open, visible, and permanent when you bought your home, you may have taken your property subject to that encroachment. You can't turn around a few years later and demand that it be removed. The neighbor has an **implied easement** on your property to continue using it in that manner.

If the encroachment is less obvious, you may only discover it when you have a survey conducted for some other purpose. What to do? You have several options.

- Demand that the neighbors remove the encroachment. If they refuse, you could file a quiet title lawsuit or ejection lawsuit and obtain a court order requiring removal. Of course, this approach isn't the best for neighborly feelings, especially if the fixture in question is the cornice of his house. Further, if prior owners of the neighboring property have used that bit of your land for quite a few years, your current neighbor could ask a court to declare a prescriptive easement to keep doing so (see above).

- Sell the strip of land to your neighbors. Perhaps you didn't know quite where the boundary line was anyway, so you might as well agree on a new one on your side of the encroachment and file it with the county recording office.

- Grant written permission to use your land in that way. This maneuver can actually ward off a claim for prescriptive easement or adverse possession, because perfecting either of these claims requires showing that the use was open and hostile (without permission). If you like this neighbor but may not like those who follow, you might grant permission only as long as that neighbor owns the property. Your attorney could draw up a document granting permission and file it for you.

The primary question when someone has encroached a bit onto your property is how important it really is to you. Typically, disputes over encroachments arise when there's already dissension between neighbors. If everyone's getting along fine, chances are you can live quite happily even though your neighbors' fence does stand a foot or two on your side of the line. Choose the least contentious option and get on with your life.

BOLTS FROM THE BLUE

Earlier we looked at title insurance as a stockade fence around your title, protecting you from several types of surprise attacks. By now it's clear that the protection is only partial; title insurance won't cover a wide range of encumbrances that the company specifically excludes.

Nor will it help if you're struck by a bolt from the blue: a challenge to your ownership that arises after closing. In addition to court judgments, divorce decrees, mechanic's liens, unpaid assessments, and other problems we've already covered, here are two other challenges that you'd best know about.

Eminent Domain

Since ancient times, governments have had the right to obtain private property for governmental purposes. This power, called **eminent domain**, is practically universal. But in the United States this power is limited by the Bill of Rights, which grants people the right to due process of law and just compensation if they're deprived of their property.

The federal government and individual states may delegate their condemnation power to municipalities, highway authorities, forest preserve districts, public utilities, and others. These authorities may force the purchase of private land for public purposes, whether building a new freeway or expanding a school playground.

If the government wants your land, you may hear about it informally at a public hearing on the matter. Chances are you and your neighbors won't be happy about it. You can't stop a condemnation by arguing that the proposed use isn't a public purpose because the scope of government's activity has expanded so much in recent years that almost anything counts as a public purpose. Your best approach would be rallying the neighbors to city hall in hopes of influencing the plans—perhaps making the new road narrower so it doesn't take people's front yards.

Your first official notice will be a letter indicating interest in acquiring your property (or a portion of it) for a given purpose. That's when informal negotiations should kick into high gear. With or without your input, the government then has your property appraised and makes you an offer, called the ***pro tanto award***. You may accept it or refuse it. If you accept it, the government may ask you to sign a document waiving your right to sue for more. Some government agencies offer a bonus to entice people into accepting the *pro tanto* award, because paying a bonus is cheaper than going to court.

In a typical project, about 75 percent of the property owners accept the government's initial offer. The rest sue for more, but three quarters of them settle the case before trial.

IF THE GOVERNMENT WANTS YOUR PROPERTY

The good news is that your city is finally going to have a new fire station. The bad news is that it's slated for your land.

Governments have a legal right to condemn your property for public purposes, which means they can require you to sell it. Although you can try to influence the plans, ultimately your only power is deciding how much money you're willing to accept for your home and the inconvenience of moving. The government wants to obtain the land for as low a price as possible, so don't expect its officials to look out for your interests.

If you refuse the government's initial offer, determining the selling price is often a matter of negotiation. Your best ally is an attorney with plenty of experience in matters of eminent domain, because someone who knows the ropes can probably secure a much higher price for you. Call the local bar association for a reference.

Some eminent domain lawyers work on a contingency basis, taking as their fee a given percentage of the difference between the initial offer and the ultimate settlement. You might want to set up a fee arrangement where you pay a flat fee or hourly rate for initial review, negotiation, and counteroffer, then switch to contingent fee if the matter turns into a lawsuit. In some areas you are entitled to attorney's fees if you have to sue and wind up with more than what's offered by the state.

If you don't think the offer is high enough, retain a lawyer experienced in eminent domain cases to negotiate for you and prepare your case for possible trial (see box, above). If the case does go to trial, it's a battle of experts. Each side brings in various expert witnesses to testify to the value of the property, which is ultimately set by the jury. If you're lucky, you'll get enough to buy a new house with fewer aggravations than the one you lost.

Property Seizures

In cases of eminent domain the federal government is scrupulous about due process of law; but in a different and relatively new area statutes give the government far more leeway. If the police suspect you of certain kinds of crime (e.g., drug dealing), the law allows them to seize any of your property that might have been used in the commission of the crime or purchased with proceeds from the crime.

You might also be in trouble if police suspect others of using your property for illegal purposes. For instance, if your tenant grows marijuana in the basement of your rental house, the police might seize the house, sell it, and keep the equity to fund further law-enforcement efforts. Since 1985, law-enforcement officials have seized more than $2.6 billion worth of houses, cash, cars, and other assets.

What disturbs many critics is that for civil forfeitures, the owner doesn't have to be convicted of a crime. However, as a result of a 1993 Supreme Court decision, government officials are generally no longer free to seize property without warning if they believe it can be linked to criminal activity. Now authorities have to give the property owner notice and an opportunity to be heard, except in exigent circumstances.

The value of the property forfeited need have no relation to the seriousness of the crime, as an Iowa man learned when he lost his $6,000 boat because he caught three fish illegally.

In a California case, a couple held a second mortgage on a house that was occupied by a businessman convicted of running an interstate prostitution ring. Federal agents seized the house and kept it for five years while it fell into disrepair. The owners had to go to court to regain their property.

A growing number of critics are calling for legal reform in this area. In the meantime, better make sure there's not even an appearance of criminal activity in any house or vehicle you own. If your property does get seized by the government, retain a knowledgeable, assertive lawyer as fast as you can.

■

CHAPTER FOUR

Fire! Thief! Asbestos!

Protecting Your Home and Your Health

THE STORIES ON THE EVENING NEWS could break your heart. A couple who saved for years to buy their own mobile home starts picking up the pieces after a tornado levels their neighborhood. A burglar breaks into someone's lovely house and steals the family's Christmas presents. A farmer with little to spare watches his homestead burn to the ground. Two children living in a beautiful old house suffer lead poisoning from the dust in the air and can't remember their own names.

Many of the perils that could befall your home come suddenly and unexpectedly from the outside. For some of these you can take steps to minimize loss, such as making sure your woodstove is properly installed and using deadbolts on your doors. For others, from tornadoes to floods to riots, there's not much you can do. That's why you need the best homeowners' insurance policy you can afford.

Other perils are more insidious because they come from the inside. Asbestos around the furnace, lead dust in the air, bacteria in the well, radon in the basement—these are all hidden dangers. Although they can pose a serious threat to the health of everyone in your household, your homeowner's policy won't pay for testing and removal.

This chapter will look at a range of perils, exterior and interior, with suggestions on reducing your risk and making sure you'll have enough money to start over should the next sad story on the evening news be yours.

Let's begin with homeowners' insurance because it's one protection you need to have before you move in—in fact, before you can even get a loan to buy the house in the first place. Your lending institution requires a certain level of coverage to protect its interest, but don't assume that level will protect yours as well. After all, the lender only wants to make sure there'll be enough money to pay off the loan if the house burns down. You want enough to rebuild the house and replace all the furniture, clothes, and appliances you lost in the fire.

That's a big difference. Make sure you understand what your policy covers and what it doesn't. Buy enough insurance to cover the losses you might suffer.

Broadly speaking, a homeowners' policy is a package deal designed to pay for the repair or replacement of your house and belongings, plus extra living expenses if, say, you and your family have to stay in a motel for several months while your home is being rebuilt. It also covers claims and legal judgments against you for injuries people suffer in your home or for damage you cause. How much the insurer pays depends, of course, on the limits of your policy, which in turn depend on how much you've paid in premiums. (For more on the liability provisions of your homeowners' policy, see chapter 5.)

Although policy details vary from company to company, the general forms of coverage are fairly standard. The cheapest coverage, called HO-1 or "basic form," is so limited that many companies don't even offer it. It pays only if the damage is caused by eleven specific perils, including fire or lightning, windstorm or hail, explosion, smoke, or theft. If your pipes burst or your roof collapses under a load of ice, you won't be covered. HO-2 or "broad form" covers these and a few other stated perils.

A form called "special," or HO-3, is actually the most common as well as the best, because although coverage of your possessions is limited to the same perils listed for HO-2, the house itself is covered for all perils except a few that are specifically excluded, such as flood, earthquake, war, and nuclear accident. Get it if you can afford it, because you never know what might happen.

If you live in a condo or cooperative, an HO-6 policy gives you coverage similar to HO-2. A few companies do offer all-risk coverage for condo and co-op owners. As with any other type of significant purchase, it pays to shop around.

What if you live in a historic house? Insurers are leery of special old houses because they're prone to faulty wiring and ruptured plumbing, and repairs are very expensive and replacement nearly impossible. The best you're likely to get for your grand old Victorian is an HO-8 policy, which doesn't cover damage caused by wiring or plumbing failures. Your coverage is based on market value, not the cost of rebuilding. And if a windstorm blows out the stained-glass windows, the policy may only pay for plain new ones.

Even an all-risk policy has a number of exceptions. Policies differ, but chances are yours excludes:

- water damage, including floods, sewer backups, and seepage from ground water
- damage you do deliberately
- earthquakes, unless you buy a special rider
- damage from the house settling
- damage from a continuous plumbing or heating leak, rather than a sudden one
- separate business or rental structures on the property
- damage by birds, rodents, insects, or family pets
- loss or vandalism if you've abandoned the house for thirty days or more
- normal wear and tear

Typically your policy includes up to 50 percent of the policy's limit for personal property, up to 20 percent for outbuildings (such as a garage, coach house, or toolshed) and another 20 percent for interim living expenses. So if you insured your house for $200,000, you'd get $100,000 for personal possessions, $40,000 for outbuildings, and $40,000 for living expenses.

If you have luxury items worth more, consider listing them on a separate schedule and insuring them individually. Standard policies cap payments for silverware at $2,500, cash and rare coins at $200, boats at $1,000, and jewelry, watches, and furs at $1,500. You can either pay a bit more and raise the limit in particular categories, or have individual items appraised, listed on a separate schedule, and insured for that amount.

If you schedule your diamond ring, you're covered even if it simply disappears, whether or not you can show a likelihood of theft. Nearly all types of damage are covered. However, you're limited to the exact amount of the appraisal, even if the ring has increased in value since then. If it has decreased in value, you may be paying for coverage you don't need. So if you schedule your valuables, be sure to have them appraised periodically to make sure you're not underinsured.

How Much Is Enough?

Until recently, home owners have often been advised to insure their home for 80 percent of its value. The idea was that total destruction of a house is relatively rare, so you're fairly safe and can save money on premiums by not insuring to full value.

Experts now stress the importance of insuring to full value. Florida's Hurricane Andrew was enough to show that people who only insure to 80 percent of value too often end up with far less than they need to rebuild.

Certainly, a home owner would be ill advised to buy any less than 80 percent. That figure is a critical cutoff point for insurers, and it can make a major difference if only part of your home is damaged. Suppose you've insured the home for only a little more than half of what it's worth, and a fire does $6,000 worth of damage to your kitchen. You won't get $6,000 from the insurance company to cover the loss. Instead, the insurer will consider the age of the house, work it into a payment formula for half-insured houses, and pay maybe $3,000 on the claim. If you insured for at least 80 percent of the home's value, the $6,000 loss from the fire would be covered in full.

The key question for the home owner is how you figure the home's value. Many people make the mistake of using their home's current market value as a guideline. But if a tornado levels your house, you'll need enough money to rebuild from the ground up—and the cost of building is nearly always higher than the cost of buying a comparable existing house in the neighborhood. Even if local real estate prices have declined, chances are the cost of building has gone up.

Especially if your house is more than thirty years old, you'll probably need an appraisal to determine the amount of coverage needed. Your insurance agent may be willing to do this for you. In case the agent or appraiser estimates wrong, though, you might want to pay a bit more and buy guaranteed replacement-cost coverage. That way you get the actual cost of rebuilding even if it's higher than the stated policy limit.

Another way to guard against underinsurance is with an **inflation guard clause**, which increases the face value of the policy either according to the annual increase in local construction costs or by a given percentage every three months. This rider can reduce the chances of your being underinsured, but it doesn't guarantee replacement cost.

You may qualify for a discount if you've taken particular safety precautions such as installing deadbolt locks or cabling your mobile home to the ground. Ask your insurance agent what discounts are available and what you'd need to do to qualify.

Check your current policy to see whether your personal possessions are insured for their actual cash value or their replacement cost. Covering for actual cash value costs less, but it's likely to lead to unpleasant surprises. In the world of insurance, actual cash value means purchase price minus depreciation.

Suppose you bought your sofa fifteen years ago for $800, and the reasonable life expectancy of a sofa of that quality is twenty years. A smoldering cigarette starts a fire that destroys the sofa. The claims adjuster might determine that three quarters of its life expectancy is past, so you're only entitled to $200. But at today's prices, it might cost you $1,000 or more to buy a new one. Replacement-cost coverage costs only 10 to 15 percent more, so it's an excellent value.

Natural Disasters

Are you covered if your home is destroyed by a hurricane, tornado, flood, earthquake, or volcano? Not necessarily. Because of the differing nature of these perils, each is treated differently by the insurance industry, and consumers are often confused about what their homeowners' policy covers and what it doesn't. On October 17, 1989, when an earthquake devastated San Francisco, only 20 percent of the home owners in the area were covered by earthquake endorsements—even though all of them surely knew they were at risk. Here's an overview of what coverage is available for specific types of disasters and how you get it.

- **Floods.** Homeowners' policies absolutely exclude damage from flooding, except for a narrow range of cases such as a pipe or water tank bursting. You can't get an endorsement to cover it at any price. However, if your community is in a flood-prone area, you can probably buy a special policy as part of the National Flood Insurance Program, administered by private insurers and backed by the federal government. Any insurance agent can sell flood policies.

  How much such a policy costs depends on what measures your community has taken to reduce the risk of flood damage. Until your community meets the standards of the federal flood-control program, you can only get limited coverage: up to $35,000 for a single-family house and $10,000 for its contents, for about $250 per year. Once the community meets the federal standards you can get up to $185,000 for a single-family house and $60,000 for its contents. The premiums depend on the structure of the house and how close it is to the river, but in a moderately flood-prone area, $60,000 of coverage on a house and its contents might cost about $150 per year.

- **Earthquakes.** The state of California requires insurance carriers to offer earthquake coverage to anyone in the state who carries one of their homeowners' policies. Usually it's an endorsement to the regular policy, expanding the coverage for a fee. But if a California policyholder decides not to buy or renew the endorsement, the carrier isn't obligated to give her a second chance.

  Of course, given the risk, earthquake endorsements in that part of the country don't come cheap. The annual premium on a $100,000 house could be anywhere from $150 to $1,200, depending on the location of the house and the materials used in its construction. Brick houses, which generally hold up the worst in earthquakes, would be at the high end of the spectrum.

  Deductibles on earthquake endorsements are usually 10 percent of the coverage for the structure and its contents, figured separately. So even if you have $50,000 worth of earthquake coverage on your Silicon Valley home, the first $5,000 worth of damage comes out of your own pocket.

In other parts of the country you can get earthquake endorsements, often for next to nothing—but most people don't because they don't expect to need them.

- **Tornadoes and hurricanes.** Although standard homeowners' policies cover windstorms, you may need extra protection if you live in an area such as Florida or Texas that's especially prone to hurricanes or tornados. In these areas, standard coverage may not be available; you have to buy a special policy such as the beach-and-windstorm insurance plans available in seven Atlantic and Gulf Coast states. As with flood insurance, any licensed agent or broker in those states can sell it.

- **Volcanoes.** Until Mt. St. Helens erupted in 1980, causing millions of dollars in property damage, Americans didn't think about coverage for damage caused by volcanoes. After some confusion, insurers decided to allow coverage under the standard "explosion" peril, and they paid some $27 million in claims from that eruption. Now, volcanoes are specifically listed as a covered peril in standard homeowners' policies, so there's one natural disaster you don't have to worry about.

How to File a Claim

The claims process for theft or damage to your home or its contents is fairly straightforward—and it'll go smoothly if you've taken time beforehand to take inventory of your possessions and what they're worth (see box, page 62).

- In case of burglary, first call the police.
- Then, whatever the loss, call your agent or company right away. Ask whether you're covered, whether the claim exceeds your deductible, how long it'll take to process the claim, and whether you'll need to get estimates for repairs.
- Follow up with a written explanation of what happened.

TAKING INVENTORY

If your house burned down tomorrow, would you be able to provide your agent with an itemized list of what was in it and how much it was worth? Probably not.

Although you don't need a detailed inventory to buy insurance, and you can eventually get a sizable check from the insurance company without one, the claims adjusting process goes a lot more smoothly if you have clear, accurate records.

The time-honored method is to fill in a "household inventory" booklet available from your agent, recording purchase dates of furniture, equipment, and valuables and estimating replacement costs. It helps to attach bills of sale, canceled checks, or appraisal records. The more detail you can include, the better.

Another option is to use a software package designed to categorize records of personal possessions and make it easy to update them. Some of these programs can print out the records room by room, in case of partial damage to your house.

For a visual record, consider either photographs or a videotaped tour of your house, complete with commentary. Include the insides of closets and cabinets, and take close-ups of computers, jewelry, and other valuables.

If the only copy of this inventory is in your house, it could easily be destroyed by whatever wrecks the rest of your possessions. Send a copy to your attorney, store it in a safe-deposit box, or leave it with a friend, but be sure to have a backup in a safe place.

- If needed, make temporary repairs to secure your home or keep the rain from pouring in. Keep track of expenses, as your policy will reimburse you. But don't make permanent repairs until the claims adjuster has inspected the damage.

- Prepare a detailed list of lost or damaged items. If you have to find temporary housing, save your receipts.

If you're dissatisfied with the way your adjuster handles your claim, first talk to your agent. If that doesn't help, call the company's consumer affairs department. Then try the National Insurance Consumer Helpline, 800-942-4242, which might be able

SHOPPING FOR INSURANCE

Whether you're buying your first policy or shopping for better price and coverage, begin by listing what you have and estimating its value. Get your house appraised, either by an insurance representative or by an independent appraiser, to figure out what it would cost to rebuild at current prices. Note valuables that might require special coverage.

Bone up on the types of policies available so you know what you're looking for (see pages 55–58).

Check the Yellow Pages or ask friends or relatives to recommend companies or agents who provide good service. Talk with several different agents about your insurance needs. Ask them to quote premium costs with higher and lower deductibles. Compare costs and coverages.

Check the reputation of the companies you're considering. Rating services such as A.M. Best & Co., Moody's Investor Services, Standard & Poor's Corporation, and Duff & Phelps study companies' financial stability and ability to pay claims. Your insurance agent would have the latest ratings for the companies he or she works with. Ask your agent to help you interpret the ratings scales, which vary between the services and can be confusing. You want to be reasonably sure your insurer will be in shape to pay your claim. Watch out for policies that limit recovery on personal possessions to "four times the actual cash value," which could mean you'd get less than you need to replace your houseful of old furniture and drapes. Also stay away from policies that only reimburse you for what the insurance company would be able to pay for a given item, because the company could probably buy it wholesale.

Keep your agent informed of additions to your house and major purchases that might affect the level of coverage you need. Periodically review your coverage to make sure you're adequately insured.

to suggest a course of action. Finally you could call your state's insurance department to complain and ask for help.

If none of these approaches brings a satisfactory settlement, consider hiring an independent adjuster for an appraisal of your damage. You'll have to pay a fee of 10 to 15 percent of your final settlement. Check with your state insurance department, though, to find out whether public adjusters have to be licensed in your state. Don't do business with someone at your door after a loss who claims to be an adjuster; there are scam artists out there eager to take advantage of your misfortune. If necessary, you could insist on arbitration of the dispute with your insurance carrier. An independent arbitrator selected by the attorneys for both sides will hear the arguments and decide what compensation you're entitled to. For the name of an arbitration organization near you, contact Arbitration Forums, P.O. Box 217500, Tampa, Florida, 33688-1500, 800-967-8889; or the American Arbitration Association, 212-484-4000.

For disputes involving just a few thousand dollars, it's probably cheaper to present your own case in small claims court. (See box, pages 114–115, for more information.)

FENDING OFF INTRUDERS

Nothing can make a home owner feel so violated as to have a burglar break in and rifle through private possessions. That is, unless the intruder comes after you and your family. The fact that your homeowners' insurance will probably cover the cost of replacing what's taken is small comfort when your sense of security is cut to shreds.

There's less danger if the intruder is of the four-legged variety, whether deer in the vegetable garden or skunks under the woodpile. But these uninvited guests can be troublesome too, and in some cases can cause considerable damage.

In either case, the first line of defense is preventing unwanted entry in the first place. Both humans and animals can often be deterred by a few simple measures.

If your barriers fail, it's a good idea to know what you can and can't do legally to fend off intruders.

Keeping Burglars Out

Most burglars aren't professionals; most are young, inexperienced, scared, and looking for easy money. So you can do a lot to protect yourself and your things by using a burglar's worse enemies: time, light, and noise. If breaking into your house takes a long time, involves working in the light, or creates a lot of noise, a burglar will probably go somewhere else.

Although you may not be able to keep intruders out indefinitely, most give up if they're delayed four or five minutes. A professional criminal intent on getting in may not be deterred no matter what you do, but the majority will probably be deterred by a few simple measures. (See box, page 66, for specifics.)

Beware of scam artists who come selling home-security systems, using scare tactics to get you to shell out. Some sell worthless steel doors that can be pushed in, some insist that a simple device will make your home safe, and some overcharge for products you could get at your local hardware store. Watch out or you really will be robbed—by the crook selling the system.

If There's an Intruder in Your House

"Honey, did you hear a noise downstairs?" Everyone's afraid of finding someone in the house at night. If it happens to you, do all you can to avoid a confrontation. Your life is more important than your stuff.

- Run away if you can and call police.
- If you can't get yourself and your family out of the house, lock yourselves in a room.
- If you're face to face with an intruder, stay calm and be cooperative.

What about using force?

You do have a legal right to protect yourself and your property. Some home owners keep a gun handy for just such an occasion, although more people get shot with their own guns than use them to frighten off or disable intruders. If you did shoot an intruder or whack him over the head with an iron pipe—then found yourself in court on assault charges—you could argue that you acted in self-defense or in defense of your property. It would be up to the jury to decide whether to believe you.

Basically, the law says you can use reasonable force to defend yourself if you're being attacked or if you have a reasonable belief that you will be. That is, you don't have to wait until the

A CHECKLIST ON HOME SECURITY

How easy would it be for a crook to get into your home? Experts advise home owners to begin by casing their place the way a burglar would. Identify the easiest place to get in and make it harder.

- *Are there exterior lights on the front and back sides?*
- *Are there shrubs around your doors and windows that a burglar could use for cover? Better trim them.*
- *Do you have a privacy fence that could give burglars privacy, too?*
- *Do you have deadbolt locks on your doors? Do you keep them locked, even if you're out working in the yard?*
- *Are your doors solid, at least 1¼ inch thick, and do they fit snugly in the frame?*
- *Have you installed a specially designed lock for your sliding glass door?*
- *Could a burglar slide a window open from the outside and climb in? If you have double-hung windows, a removable nail pinning the upper and lower halves together is quite effective.*
- *Should you consider grates for your street-level windows? Be aware that they can trap you inside in case of fire.*
- *Would an alarm go off if an intruder stepped inside? Burglars hate noise. A sticker on your window declaring you have an alarm system may be enough to scare off some would-be intruders (whether you actually have an alarm or not).*
- *Do you ever leave your house keys with your car keys when you have your car parked?*
- *Do you carry house keys on a key ring with a name-and-address tag?*
- *Do you hide a key in a secret place outside your home? Burglars know where to look.*
- *When you go on vacation, could strangers tell that you're gone? Don't let mail and newspapers pile up outside, and make sure your lawn stays mowed and your walks stay shoveled. Use automatic timers for lights and a radio. Leave your blinds open, in their usual position.*

intruder is actually coming at you with a knife. The key word here is *reasonable*; the jury would have to decide whether a reasonable person would have thought that the toy gun was real or that the hand going into the pocket was reaching for a weapon. States vary widely on what they consider "reasonable force." In general, if you use force against an intruder, use no more than appears necessary. That is, if a shout sends the burglar running, don't pull a gun and shoot him in the back. If a single blow stops a burglar in his tracks, don't beat him to a pulp. If the intruder isn't threatening bodily harm to someone in the house, you're on shaky ground if you use deadly force.

Some courts have held that a home owner who could retreat safely isn't justified in beating or killing the intruder. Likewise, courts have held that a home owner isn't justified in attacking a burglar if it appears that a shout or warning would be enough.

What about booby-trapping your home to keep burglars out? Despite the popularity of the movie *Home Alone*, people have gotten into serious legal trouble for that sort of thing. Even if you're fed up with repeated break-ins, you can't set up a gun rigged to shoot anyone who comes through the window. It's not up to you to impose a death sentence on someone who might try to break in. And the next person through the window might be a firefighter trying to save you.

Animal Intruders

It's lovely to see deer from your kitchen window—unless they're busy tearing up your vegetable garden. And you'd probably be delighted to hear woodpeckers or sapsuckers rapping in search of grubs, but not if they were drilling holes in your cedar siding. People move to wooded areas partly because they enjoy living so close to wildlife, but beavers do have their own idea of the proper way to manage an aspen grove.

What can you do? It depends on the animal. Your state department of fish and wildlife has jurisdiction over wild critters; a call to the nearest office will probably get you some advice. If the animal in question is something large and potentially dangerous like a bear in your apple tree, the agency may send someone out to trap the animal and take it somewhere else. Otherwise, they may invite you down to pick up a trap and learn how to use it yourself.

In some cases you may be able to convince the critters to stay away from your property. A fence eight feet high will keep most deer out, though they've been known to jump one even that high. Dried blood scattered around seems to repel rabbits, and birds are less likely to fly into a window if there's a silhouette of a falcon taped to it. To a certain extent, though, people who choose to live with nature have to get used to nature living with them.

What if things are getting out of hand? Farmers lose thousands of dollars of crops to deer, pronghorns, and other graceful neighbors. In the West, ranchers have to cope with marauding bears and coyotes. For some, the simplest solution may appear to be a little preseason hunting. State officials look askance on that sort of thing, though, even if it's done in an attempt to protect property. You can be convicted of killing wildlife without a permit, an offense that often carries a hefty fine. Many states do assist farmers with reducing the damage, and some reimburse farmers and ranchers for wildlife damage. Note that reimbursement programs, which are funded by hunting license fees, aren't open to farmers who bar hunters from their land.

Broadly speaking, before you can protect your property by killing game animals out of season or without a permit, you must have taken all reasonable steps to alleviate the problem. These may include opening your land to hunters in season, trying reasonable suggestions from the game warden, trapping animals, and hazing them. But many states allow killing of gophers, rattlesnakes, and coyotes without a permit.

What about a dog attacking your chickens? The owner of one Labrador retriever sued her neighbor for blasting the dog with a shotgun after it killed eleven chickens and was cornering the last one. She claimed that the dog was worth $3,500 and shouldn't have been killed to protect a $2.50 chicken. The court rejected her argument and awarded the neighbor $30 for the cost of his chickens, ruling that killing a dog in defense of property is reasonable if the danger is imminent and there's no other way to stop it. In general, though, it's best to use only as much force as necessary to stop the damage. If nothing else, that will help you get along with your neighbors.

HOME, TOXIC HOME

Toxic home? That's not an appealing thought, but for many home owners it's right on target. A home can look and smell perfectly fine, yet have deadly lead dust in the air, cancer-causing radon in the basement, and an abandoned oil tank under the front yard leaching oil into the water table. Although toxic waste regulations apply to home owners just the same as to businesses (see below), there are no laws requiring asbestos, lead, and other contaminants to be removed from private homes. It's a matter of health and safety for you and your family.

In some cases, you may find out about one of these problems when a painter points out the lead-based paint on your woodwork or a remodeling contractor finds asbestos around the furnace and won't proceed until it's removed. You might learn about lead the hard way when your children can't think straight, or about contaminated water when the whole family gets sick. Health problems from asbestos or radon, though, won't show up for another thirty years. The only way to discover and correct the problem may be to hire an expert to conduct the right tests.

In a growing number of states, sellers are required by law to inform potential buyers if they know about asbestos or other toxic substances in the house. Then it's up to the buyer and seller to work out who's responsible for dealing with it. The seller might lower the price to compensate the buyer for having to cope with the problem.

In other states, the general rule is "buyer beware." A seller can't set out to misrepresent or hide the condition or lie if asked, but there's no obligation to disclose the problem. These days, though, home buyers often make the offer contingent on a satisfactory result of testing. Regular home inspectors aren't usually qualified to test for lead or radon, so getting an accurate test would require hiring a qualified specialist. The down side is that too many layers of testing can make a seller lose patience.

If you learn that your house has a lot of asbestos or lead and the prior owner didn't tell you, can you make the prior owner help pay for removal? Maybe, if you live in a state that requires disclosure *and* you can prove that the prior owner knew about the problem.

It's not easy, though, to find out what someone knew and when, and to prove it in court. A bit of detective work might uncover, say, a furnace contractor who advised the owner of the problem a year before, drew up a recommendation, and heard the owner say not to bother because he was going to sell the place soon. But that's unlikely. Really, it comes down to what it's worth to pursue the matter. The kind of person who'll deceive you about a health problem in the house you'll be living in isn't likely to volunteer to hand over thousands of dollars to fix the problem now that he doesn't own the house. So the only way to recover would be to get a lawyer and threaten a lawsuit—and be willing to carry through. But if it costs $10,000 to remove the asbestos from your house, is it worth a $15,000 lawsuit to recover the cost?

If you're worried about radon, asbestos, lead, or other household toxins, be careful about who you hire to test and deal with it. Whatever the latest scare, there are scam artists ready to prey on the unwary. They may show up on our doorstep offering to test your house and save your life, for a sizable fee. But chances are they don't have the proper training to do the job right, even if it does need to be done.

For instance, people claiming to be asbestos consultants and contractors may find asbestos and try to convince you that it must be removed right away, even though the proper treatment for asbestos in many cases is to leave it in place (see asbestos section below). Then they'll remove it unnecessarily, which is a waste of money, and do so improperly, which can increase the health risk.

To avoid such scams, bone up on the nature of each home toxin, what services are available, and what procedures and precautions the job involves to be done right. For names of licensed professionals in your area, check state or local health departments or EPA regional offices. As with any home improvements contractor, ask for references from previous clients, make sure the contractor has completed similar projects, and get estimates from more than one. (See chapter 6 for more on checking out contractors.)

Asbestos

Asbestos is a fibrous material found in rocks and soils world-wide. Because it's strong, durable, fire resistant, and effective as an insulator, until the early 1970s it was widely used in flooring, walls, shingles, ceiling tiles, and insulation or fire retardant for furnaces and wiring.

Unfortunately, repeated long-term exposure to this wonderful stuff causes cancer and lung disease. When the material crumbles or flakes, tiny asbestos flakes escape into the air. When the fibers are inhaled, they remain in the lungs, and repeated exposure can lead to lung disease.

If the asbestos-containing material is in good shape and not likely to be disturbed, it may be best to leave it in place. But if it's going to be scraped, hammered, sawed, or otherwise disturbed, better get a trained professional to find a way to minimize dissemination.

Since total removal is expensive and difficult, intermediate options include applying a sealant or covering the asbestos with a protective wrap or jacket. It's tricky business, and even the cleanup needs to be done with a special vacuum cleaner to avoid scattering asbestos fibers. Don't try any of this yourself. Make sure the contractors you hire don't track asbestos through the house or break the old material into small pieces.

To avoid conflict of interest, anyone you hire to survey your house for asbestos shouldn't be connected to an asbestos correction firm. The federal government has training courses for asbestos consultants and contractors, and so do some state and local governments. Ask to see documentation proving that everyone working with asbestos in your home has completed state or federal training.

Lead

Lead is a soft, metallic element occurring naturally in rocks and soil all over the world. Until fairly recently it was commonly used in pipes, plumbing solder, paint, and gasoline. Inhaling particles of lead dust or drinking water contaminated with lead causes lead to accumulate in blood, bones, and soft tissue. High concentrations of lead can cause permanent damage to the brain, central nervous system, kidneys, and red blood cells. It's especially dangerous for infants, children, pregnant women, and the unborn because the sensitive tissues of growing bodies absorb lead more easily. Also, a given concentration of lead has worse effects on a child's smaller body than on an adult's.

- **Lead in drinking water.** Lead-based solder has been banned since 1988, but homes built before then often have lead-solder joints that corrode into drinking water. You can't tell whether pipes leach lead by looking at them, but a simple chemical test can make that determination. If you want to have your water tested, ask your local, county, or state health or environment department about qualified testing laboratories.

  If you're having plumbing work done in an older home, check for lead pipes and make sure the plumber doesn't use lead solder. Even new faucets and fixtures can put some lead into the water. One way to reduce the risk is to run the faucet for fifteen seconds before drinking the water.

  If you do have lead in your water, several means are available to reduce corrosion, including calcite filters, distillation units, and reverse-osmosis devices. Water softeners and carbon, sand, or cartridge filters are not effective for removing lead. Get qualified advice before buying or leasing any device, as effectiveness varies from one kind to another.

- **Lead-based paint** was applied to some two thirds of the houses built before 1940 and to a third of those built between 1940 and 1960, according to the EPA. Lead paint tastes sweet, so children have been poisoned from chewing on flakes of paint. Lead dust is stirred up when woodwork painted with lead-based paint is scraped, sanded, or heated with an open flame stripper. Then the lead dust settles in fibers and fabric and can be stirred up again by normal cleaning.

  The only accurate way to tell whether your house has lead-based paint is to remove a sample and have it tested by a qualified laboratory. Contact a local, county, or state health or environmental department about where to find one.

If lead-based paint is in good condition and there's not much chance it'll be nibbled on by children, it's best to leave it alone. Otherwise, you can cover it with wallpaper or some other building material or completely replace the woodwork. Removing lead paint properly and safely is a time-consuming and expensive process that requires residents to leave the house during removal and cleanup.

If the exterior of the house was painted before 1950, the surrounding soil is probably contaminated with lead. Don't leave patches of bare soil, and clean your floors and windowsills regularly with wet rags and mops. Everyone in the family should wash their hands frequently.

Radon

Radon is a colorless, odorless, tasteless gas resulting from the natural decay of uranium in the earth. It comes into your house through small cracks, floor drains, wall/floor joints, and the pores in hollow block walls, and it tends to accumulate in the lowest level of the home. It can also get trapped in ground water, so homes with wells are more likely to have a radon problem. Radon particles lodge in the lungs, where they break down and release bursts of radiation that can damage lung tissue and cause cancer.

Testing for radon in well water requires sending a sample to a laboratory for analysis. Inexpensive test kits for radon in the air are available at hardware stores, but be sure they've been approved by a federal or state health, environmental, or consumer protection agency. Long-term testing over a year is most accurate, but short-term testing can let you know if you have a potential problem.

If rooms in your house register more than four picocuries of radon per liter of air, the radon should be reduced. This normally isn't a do-it-yourself project, but professional radon-reduction contractors can determine the source of the gas and then seal leaks and install fans, pumps, or other equipment to keep it out. Special filter systems can remove radon from your water supply. Depending on the number of sources, the amount of radon, and the construction of the home, installing radon-reduction equipment costs anywhere from several hundred to several thousand dollars.

Toxic Waste

When we think of toxic waste, we usually think of big chemical companies, nuclear reactors, or old mine tailings. But a residential property can also be a toxic waste site, potentially dangerous to the home owner and the neighbors. Most family farms have a ravine or back lot that's long been a handy place to dump all kinds of things, including old pesticide containers that haven't necessarily been rinsed out according to label instructions. And a private home may have a leaky heating oil tank buried under the back yard, either one still in use or an abandoned one that was never emptied when the heating system was converted to natural gas.

Oil, pesticides, or other toxic substances from these sources can leak fumes into a neighbor's basement, contaminate nearby wells, or migrate through the water table until there's an oil slick on the nearest creek.

The law may hold home owners responsible for the cost of cleaning up toxic waste sites, whether or not they had anything to do with creating the problem. Responsible parties, including the current home owner, the owner of the property when the pollution was caused, and the person or company who caused it (which could be a third party altogether), are **jointly and severally** liable. "Jointly and severally" means that any one of them can be forced to pay the entire cost. That may well turn out to be the current home owner, who's probably the easiest one to find. Then it's up to the home owner to find the others and sue to recover the cost.

How do the wheels start turning? When someone discovers the problem, the city or county health department might send an investigator to conduct tests and determine the source of the pollution. The investigation alone can be expensive. Then the department may begin the process of cleaning up the site to enforce state regulations.

The cleanup process might involve ordering the home owner to hire a consultant and a remediation crew. If it's an emergency or an immediate threat to water quality, the agency may send someone in to clean it up, then sue the home owner for reimbursement. But that's a difficult process; agencies first try to get the homeowner to take care of it.

The cleanup process may involve judgment calls and negotiation. Oil in the soil from a leaking tank, for instance, will eventually degrade. Instead of hauling all the old soil out and replacing it, it might be less expensive to drill new wells. If your property has a toxic waste problem, hire an attorney experienced with environmental matters to help you. Negotiations with authorities may involve obtaining an analysis to estimate how long it will take the waste to degrade and how far and fast it's likely to migrate until then. In some cases, these negotiations become a battle of experts.

What if you don't think you should have to pay for cleanup because you didn't have anything to do with causing the pollution? Your only hope is the "innocent landowner defense," under the Superfund Amendments and Reauthorization Act of 1986, which limits the liability of a landowner who made "all appropriate inquiry" into the environmental condition of the property before buying it. That means the only way you'll be off the hook is if you had the foresight to have an environmental survey done before buying the place to see whether it was contaminated by hazardous substances. That would include a visual inspection of the property and compiling a history of past owners and their waste disposal practices, contaminant releases, and violations and other information. Chances are you didn't do that. It's the sort of thing lenders sometimes require for commercial loans because lenders can be on the hook for toxic waste sites too, but rarely is it required for homebuyers. In the end, your best hope is simply that you don't have an old toxic waste site on your property.

To prevent future problems, check with your local health authority to find out how to meet state regulations for disposal of motor oil, paint, antifreeze, and other toxic substances. Be really careful with this stuff or it can come back to haunt you.

CHAPTER FIVE

■

Floor Wax and Dog Attacks

A Home Owner's Guide to Avoiding Liability

W HAT IF YOU WAX THE FLOOR to impress your
dinner guest, but she skids across it, falls, and breaks
her hip?

What if the excavation for the dream house you're building
causes your neighbor's basement wall to cave in?

What if your new pet Doberman takes a chunk out of the
mailman's backside?

In any of these cases, you could be liable for thousands of dollars in damages. Any time someone gets hurt on your property
because of your **negligence** (carelessness), you may be legally responsible. The same applies when you or your children care-
lessly or intentionally do things that cause damage to someone
else's property.

A typical case involves someone slipping and falling, say on
an icy walkway. Other common injuries involve power lawn
mowers, swimming pools, boats, and other recreational vehicles. Home owners are liable only if a court finds them in some
way negligent (though many settle before this point if they or
their insurer believes that a court would find them negligent).

An Ounce of Prevention . . .

Thirty years ago, the injured party probably wouldn't have sought
damages, because, after all, accidents happen. At the most, the
home owner might have been asked to reimburse the injured

party's medical bills. But times have changed, and many people now feel they're entitled to full compensation when they are injured—even by friends. In today's increasingly litigious society, a dinner guest who trips over an unsecured carpet might well file a lawsuit that drags on for years.

It is important to note that 99 percent of such cases don't go to trial. Sometimes a suit is threatened but never filed, or is dropped before trial. In many other instances, the parties agree to an out-of-court settlement.

Most home owners are smart enough to carry insurance, and the insurance company generally handles any claims against the home owner. It's only when the insurer believes the claim is unreasonable that the matter is likely to land in court. Even then, the insurer will furnish the attorney and pay any damages awarded (up to the limit of the policy), along with court costs.

Still, facing a lawsuit and going to court is no fun. Lawsuits involve months of depositions, motions, and countermotions before the trial even gets started. Even after a verdict is rendered, a party may appeal and the battle can continue for years.

As a home owner, you're far better off both preventing injuries in the first place and protecting yourself with a solid insurance policy in the event the unavoidable and unexpected does occur. If you don't, your finances—and your peace of mind—may well be at risk.

The Law of Negligence and Liability

Historically the law identified four categories of people who might be injured on your property—invitees (e.g., a mail carrier), social guests (e.g., a dinner guest), licencees (e.g., someone who stops to ask directions), and trespassers (e.g., a burglar)—and the home owner's duty of care depended on the category the injured party fell into.

Today, these distinctions have all but disappeared, though in a few jurisdictions the trespasser is still in a separate legal category from "lawful" visitors. The courts in most states now hold property owners to the same standard with respect to everyone: a duty to employ reasonable care in maintaining your property and to warn people of hazards. So, for example, if you've given

A CHECKLIST FOR A SAFE HOME

- *Repair steps and railings.*
- *Cover holes.*
- *Fix uneven walkways.*
- *Install adequate lighting.*
- *Clear walkways of ice and snow as soon as possible.*
- *Be sure children do not leave toys on steps and sidewalks.*
- *Replace throw rugs that slip or bunch up.*
- *Reroute extension cords that stretch across traffic lanes.*
- *Repair frayed electrical cords.*
- *Keep poisons and other hazards out of the reach of children, even if you don't have children.*
- *Warn guests about icy conditions and other hazards.*
- *Restrain your pet.*
- *If there are children in your area, erect barriers to your swimming pool: an automatic pool cover or a tall fence with a good lock that you lock, and an alarm on the sliding glass door from your home to the pool.*
- *Keep any guns securely locked and out of sight, where children cannot see them or gain access to them.*
- *Remove nails from stored lumber; secure any lumber piles.*
- *Don't leave ladders standing against the side of the house or garage.*
- *Don't let children stand nearby when you mow the lawn.*
- *Don't let your guests drive drunk or under the influence of drugs.*
- *Anticipate safety problems and take reasonable steps to prevent harm before it occurs.*

someone permission to pick gooseberries on your property, you'd better warn the berry picker that the local gun club is holding target practice nearby.

Generally, courts hold home owners responsible only if they are in some way negligent. The law doesn't expect a home owner to guarantee that a visitor will not get hurt. People do trip over their own feet and lightning does strike. But it's your responsibility to take reasonable care to protect people from hazards that you know about. The lack of such care is called negligence.

In what circumstances might you be held liable? The following should raise red flags for you:

- If you fail to maintain your property or create a condition that may result in injury or damage to someone else's property.

- If you know about a hazard and expect people to come onto your property, but do not eliminate the hazard, erect barriers, or warn people.

- If you are not careful about hazards that might attract children.

- If your actions (or inaction) may cause damage to your neighbors' property.

Artificial Hazards

Generally courts don't hold home owners liable for injuries stemming from natural hazards such as lakes and streams, even if the one hurt is a child, unless negligence is involved. A home owner is more likely to be held responsible if the hazard was created artificially.

For instance, a man was pushing a child on a tree swing while attending a barbecue in New York. He stepped back onto a rotted plywood board covering a sewer trap, which gave way under his weight. A court found the home owners liable because they knew about the danger but made it even worse by hanging the swing where anyone pushing a child on it would have inevitably stepped on the rotted cover.

Another example occurred in Idaho where a couple was showing a prospective renter through their house, when the prospect fell down the basement stairs and was badly injured. She sued the home owners for damages because the stairway failed to meet the local building code—there was no handrail and the stair treads were of differing widths. A court ruled their ignorance of the code was no excuse and they could be held liable.

On the other hand, take the case of a Nebraska man who just

finished shoveling his driveway in the freezing mist. He was inside getting some salt to finish the job when the mail carrier slipped and fell on the driveway. The mail carrier sued, but the court ruled the home owner was blameless because he didn't create the hazard and was doing his best to eliminate it.

As these cases illustrate, the law does not expect you to anticipate every harm that might occur when people are on your property. It does expect you to exercise due care in minimizing hazards, inform visitors of potential hazards, and use common sense in maintaining your property.

Children and Attractive Nuisances

The law concerning a property owner's responsibility for children, even when they are trespassing, has changed over the years. Back in 1901, a five-year-old drowned after falling into an uncovered excavation that had filled with water. The court ruled that because the child was a trespasser and the property owners didn't know there were children around the pit, they weren't liable.

Even then, however, another legal doctrine was evolving, stemming from injuries caused to children playing on railroad turntables left unsecured in areas the public frequented. A locomotive turntable makes a fine merry-go-round, and in a series of late-nineteenth-century cases involving such injuries, the courts found the railroads negligent. Some dangerous places look like such fun that landowners should expect children to come play, the courts ruled.

The law calls them **attractive nuisances**. Even though an uninvited child wandering into your yard to inspect the swimming pool might well be a trespasser, the law says you have a special duty to erect barriers to keep children out of harm's way.

That's why the Supreme Court of Georgia recently refused to dismiss a case against the owners of a swimming pool where a two-year-old drowned. The swimming pool was in the side yard of their home on a corner lot, three blocks from an elementary school. The yard and swimming pool were unfenced, and the pool had both a diving board and playground-type slide for easy access to the water.

Many states have specific statutes requiring protective measures around a swimming pool. Failure to adhere to these safety standards would probably make you liable in case of an accident. Check with your local building officials to determine the laws in your area—and make sure you obey them.

Or take the case of the Michigan family that stopped at a private home to buy raspberries. While the adults were talking, the two preschool boys wandered into the garage, where they found a loaded gun. One shot the other. The court ruled that although home owners can't be expected to childproof their homes, those who have reason to expect children to come around—such as the couple who sold raspberries from their home—should expect children to act on childish impulses and should take steps to protect them.

The message is clear. If there's a way in, the child finds it, and he or she gets injured, you may be liable. That's why precautions such as fences, locked gates, and swimming pool covers—and good liability insurance—are so important.

Recreational Use

What if you own a lot of land and allow someone to use it for hunting, fishing, cross-country skiing, or any other recreational activity? Are you liable if the person gets hurt? Probably not. In the 1970s, virtually all states enacted **recreational use statutes**, designed to encourage people to open their land for recreational use without fear of liability. The statutes don't protect you if you charge a fee, or if you're malicious in your failure to warn of hazards—such as not telling snowmobilers there's a cable strung at neck height across their path. For more information about such statutes in your state contact a lawyer, your state's department of conservation, or the department that issues hunting and fishing licenses.

Social Host Liability

So you like to throw parties? What's your potential liability if things get out of hand and one guest picks a fight with another? Some courts have ruled that you (the host) aren't responsible for the conduct of your guests, unless your parties routinely turn into brawls. Likewise, if one of your guests is horsing around, crashes into a ceiling fixture, and slices a tendon, you likely won't be responsible.

Where you might be liable is if you let your guest drink too much, then put him into his car and send him out on the highway. That's what happened in a landmark New Jersey case, where the home owners had been drinking scotch for a couple of hours with one of the husband's subcontractors. They walked him to his car, saw him off, and called shortly to see if he'd made it home. He hadn't. Thoroughly drunk, he'd been in a head-on collision in which a woman was seriously injured. The case went to the state supreme court, which held the hosts liable.

That's a lesson worth learning. In fact, insurance companies are now offering host liquor liability policies.

Animal Attacks

Suppose your poodle attacks the delivery truck driver. Are you liable? Probably. The law holds people responsible for the actions of their pets. Most states have so-called "dog-bite statutes," holding owners legally liable for injuries inflicted by their animals. If there's no such statute in your locality, you can still be found liable under the common-law rule that owners are legally responsible if they know the animal is likely to cause harm. You may also be found liable if you violated a leash law or a requirement to keep your pets fenced.

Most dog-bite statutes eliminate the old "one-bite" rule, which essentially gave every dog one free bite because until then the owner had no reason to believe it was dangerous. However, you the owner may still defend yourself by arguing that the person injured was trespassing, breaking the law, unreasonably careless, knowingly took the risk, or provoked your dog to attack.

Many states and municipalities have enacted "vicious dog statutes," which enable an animal control officer or a judge to declare a particular dog vicious and require the owner to confine the dog securely or muzzle it in public. Some states make it illegal even to own a dog that's been declared vicious. And some cities have imposed an outright ban on certain species, such as pit bulls, which they consider inherently vicious. Also, many jurisdictions ban wild "pets," such as wolves, bears, and dangerous snakes.

If you own a dog or another animal that might injure someone, find out what the laws are in your area by calling your local animal control office. Know your pet's temperament and be careful to keep it out of the path of strangers. Keep vaccinations current, and post warning signs if you think your pet might injure someone. These should be prominent and straightforward signs—e.g., BEWARE OF DOG—so people are clearly informed of the danger involved. (However, the signs may not absolve you from liability if a child climbs into your yard or the dog gets out.)

Damage to Neighboring Property

Just as your liability for injury to people turns on the question of negligence, so does your liability for damage to someone else's property. Traditionally property owners were not responsible for damage caused by falling tree limbs and other natural occurrences on their property, but only for damage caused by artificial conditions, such as an unsecured board from your lumber pile being carried by the wind through your neighbor's plate-glass window. The current trend, though, is for courts to apply an ordinary standard of care/negligence in both cases.

So keep an eye on your trees. If there's visible rot, better take the limb off before it falls on your neighbor's new car. Maintain your property well enough that, short of a tornado or hurricane, the wind won't blow things from your place over to your neighbor's.

If you excavate near the property line and cause your neighbors' land to subside, you may be liable whether or not their house is affected. Check with a civil or geological engineer if you're planning to excavate and think you have reason to be concerned. Your builder or contractor will know of one, or you can find one yourself through the Yellow Pages.

Similarly, if changes you make to the contours of your land cause excess rain water to pour onto your neighbor's property and results in damage, you may be liable. If you're planning to change the contours of your land, ask an attorney or your local housing authority about your state law.

Other Areas of Concern

- **Damage by children.** As a rule, you're liable for injury and damage caused by your minor children, though such damage will usually be covered by your homeowners' policy. However, if your children are over thirteen and intentionally cause damage, your homeowners' policy probably won't pick up the cost. You'd better teach the kids to respect other people and their property and make sure they learn these lessons well.

- **Waterfront areas.** If you live along a river or stream, state and local laws designed to protect wildlife habitat may preclude your clearing brush or changing the lay of the land. Don't do it without checking with your state's department that deals with fish, wildlife, and parks, usually located in your state capital.

- **Pollution.** You could be liable for the cost of cleaning up pollution stemming from underground oil tanks or old dump sites on your property, whether or not you caused the problem in the first place. That's something worth looking into before you buy a piece of property, because there's not much you can do about it afterward. Ask the seller if there are any such problems, and have your attorney include a clause in your purchase agreement that covers you in the event such problems arise. If there is special concern because of the unique nature of the property, you might even consider hiring an environmental consultant.

- **Wetlands.** Federal laws govern the draining and filling of wetlands. If you have places on your property that are boggy even part of the year, avoid serious legal trouble by finding out what your responsibilities are before making changes. You might start with your state's department of environmental protection, probably located in the state capital. The federal Office of Wetlands Protection in Washington, D.C., also might be able to help.

- **Utility lines.** As a rule you're not liable for maintenance of utility lines crossing your property, but to be safe don't do anything to cause potential damage to them, such as planting fast-growing trees under them.

Comparative Negligence and Assumption of Risk

While your best defense to any charge of negligence is that you exercised due care, there are several other defenses available as well. In some cases, a jury may decide that although a home owner was partially responsible for what happened, the person injured was also partially responsible. This is called **comparative** or **contributory** negligence.

For example, if you forget to tell your house guest that you've just dug a pit in your back yard for the new septic system, and the guest decides to get a breath of fresh air and wander around in the back yard in total darkness, a jury might find both of you partly responsible for your guest's broken leg. In that case, the jury might reduce the amount of the damage award you might otherwise have to pay.

In other cases, the jury might decide to absolve you of any responsibility because of what the law calls **assumption of risk**. For instance, when a Georgia home owner and his neighbor were trying to get rid of a nest of wasps, the neighbor climbed a ladder and sprayed the nest with insecticide. The wasps swarmed out, and the frightened neighbor fell off the ladder. Then he sued the home owner for the resulting injuries. The court ruled that the neighbor knew perfectly well that wasps tend to swarm, yet assumed the risk. Accordingly, the home owner wasn't liable.

In Case of Injury

Until now, the discussion has centered on what to do to avoid hazards in and around your home. But what do you do if someone is injured on your property?

First and foremost, do all you can to help—express concern, ask what injuries might have been suffered, make the victim as comfortable as possible, call for medical assistance, etc.

Do not, however, say anything to suggest or admit guilt or negligence. While it is natural to feel bad for the injured party and want to soothe any pain and suffering, as well as your own feelings of guilt, it is not a good idea to complicate your potential liability with such statements.

Rather, it's up to the law to decide who's responsible. Notify your insurer in writing (and speak to your attorney) as soon as possible, and don't talk with the other party or his attorney about liability until you have taken these steps. You may well decide later to offer to defray some medical bills for the injured party, but do this after you have had the chance to review the situation with a clearer head and the appropriate parties.

There is one other situation in which the law requires you to act. If someone has been hurt on your property or is in danger, you may have a legal duty to offer humanitarian aid even though you had nothing at all to do with the injury. For instance, a Minnesota cattle buyer became severely ill while inspecting a farmer's cattle. A court later ruled that the farmer had a duty not to send the man, who was helpless and fainting, out on the road alone on a cold winter night.

Liability Insurance

Given your potential liability, you are asking for trouble if you do not carry adequate liability insurance. Without adequate insurance, it only takes one person seriously injured by your negligence to generate a huge liability award and deplete your financial nest egg, not to mention your psychological well-being.

The liability portion of your homeowners' policy is designed to cover unintentional injuries on the premises and unintentional damage to other people's property—in other words, injuries caused by your negligence are covered, but not injuries inflicted on purpose.

A typical homeowners' policy includes $100,000 of liability insurance, which won't go far if someone is severely injured. For a slight increase in premium you can raise that to $300,000 or $500,000, and some companies offer $1 million or more. The coverage includes harm caused by your children and pets, except intentional harm if the child is over thirteen. If your pet attacks people routinely, the insurer may cancel your policy or refuse to renew it.

Most standard homeowners' policies *don't* cover:

- Employees and clients of your home-based business, including the children in your home-based day care if you take in more than three children and have no special endorsement
- Claims by one member of the household against another
- Any disease you pass on to someone

If you have a home-based business that involves people coming to your house, be sure to obtain a separate business rider. And if you have a swimming pool or other special hazard, check the policy provisions to make sure you're covered.

If you have domestic employees—even part-time ones such as nannies—you may be required to carry workers' compensation insurance, which costs a little over $100 per year. Workers' compensation sets limits on awards; if you don't have it, you could have to pay far larger damages. And there may be civil and criminal penalties if you don't carry it. Contractors working on your house should already have workers' compensation for their employees. You should ask to see proof of such coverage, and don't hire them if they don't produce sufficient verification or don't have adequate coverage.

Umbrella Coverage

What if someone gets so badly hurt on your property that the liability portion of your homeowners' policy doesn't cover your resulting costs? That's when you'd be glad to have an umbrella liability policy, sometimes called a "personal excess liability" policy. This would protect you in case of a big judgment that would quickly eat up your regular policy coverage.

These policies are relatively inexpensive because the insurers are betting you'll never need to file a claim. Their coverage takes up where your home and auto policies leave off, so in order to obtain one you have to have certain levels of basic home and auto liability insurance—generally $100,000 in liability coverage on your homeowners' policy and $250,000/$500,000 on your auto ($250,000 per person, $500,000 per accident; or sometimes $300,000 in single-limit coverage).

You also have to meet certain eligibility requirements, such as owning no more than four cars. If you've been convicted for driving under the influence of alcohol in the past three years, you are not likely to be approved for coverage.

Some umbrella policies pay the deductible amount that isn't covered by basic policies. Others impose a deductible, called a "retained limit," in certain circumstances. For instance, if your homeowners' policy doesn't cover slander or libel (most don't without a special endorsement), an umbrella policy with a retained limit might require you to pay the first $250 of a judgment for slander. The other kind would pay from dollar one.

Most umbrella policies don't cover injuries you cause with your motorcycle and certain watercraft, such as high-powered speedboats.

Your premium for the umbrella policy will be determined based on the number of houses, rental units, and vehicles you own. If you have one house and two cars, a typical premium costs $100 to $150 for $1 million in coverage. You will get $2 million in coverage for only about $50 to $100 more in premium costs.

People usually determine their need for umbrella liability coverage not so much by how many hazards there are on their property as by the assets they have to protect. After all, the wealthier you are, the more you have to lose if someone is injured on your property. Some people buy $5 million in coverage, and some even take out umbrellas over their umbrellas. Consult your insurance agent for help in deciding what type and amount of coverage is best for you.

CHAPTER SIX

■

Remodeling?

How to Avoid Getting Nailed

THE URGE TO IMPROVE YOUR HOME is just about as irresistible as the urge to improve your spouse. But home improvement is both more likely to succeed and better protected by law.

State and federal laws frequently address remodeling because the industry is fraught with scams and shoddy workmanship. A 1992 study by the Consumer Federation of America showed that, nationwide, home repairs ranked just behind auto repairs as a source of complaints. And state consumer protection specialists in Illinois and New Jersey found that the most common consumer grievances in those states concerned home repair contracts.

Just imagine what could go wrong:

- The contractor you hire to add a second story above your living room takes your deposit and tears off the roof, but is too busy with other jobs to make further progress. It's raining.

- The kitchen remodeler brings in three subcontractors to do the work, then takes your check and skips town without paying them.

- The new swimming pool leaks, the contractor blames the plumber, and neither is willing to foot the bill for digging out the pipes.

A major remodeling brings enough headaches without trouble from an unreliable contractor. To make sure the project goes as smoothly as possible, take time to choose a reputable contractor and make sure you have a fair contract. Know your legal rights and what to do if something goes wrong.

Your Legal Rights

Both federal and state laws attempt to protect home owners who have home improvements made. Federal laws cover consumers in all states and are a big enough club that most contractors take them seriously.

Federal Trade Commission (FTC) rules address the problem of **false advertising**. It's illegal for a vendor to advertise any product or service for less than it really costs. So is the old bait-and-switch tactic, in which you are "baited" by an ad for a product or service, then told that one isn't available and "switched" to another, more expensive version. The law requires vendors to offer a rain check whenever demand for an advertised bargain exceeds supply, unless the limited supply is clearly stated in the ad.

The federal **Truth in Lending** law protects consumers who obtain outside financing for their projects. Any lender has to prominently state the annual percentage rate (APR) of interest you'll be charged. So whether you finance your home improvement through a bank, a credit union, or the contractor himself, at least you'll know what the interest rate is. It's your job to shop around for the best terms you can find.

Note that even if the terms appear reasonable, it's a bad idea to have the contractor secure financing for your project. In some areas it may also be illegal. Even though he may okay you as a credit risk when a bank won't, he has good reason: his guarantee that you'll pay him back is ultimately your house. It's probably worth a lot more than whatever you're doing to improve it. So if you can't pay for work right now, try to postpone having it done until you can.

Given the number of scam artists working the streets, your best federal protection may be the cooling-off period mandated by the Truth in Lending Act. Lawmakers were concerned about consumers being victimized by high-pressure sales pitches in their homes, perhaps because consumers relax their guard at home. Called a **right to rescission**, the law gives you three business days to cancel any contract:

- that was signed in your home (or in any location other than the seller's place of business),
- that implies any kind of financial claim to your home, as when the contract gives the contractor the right to file a lien against your home to enforce payment, and
- that involves your making four or more payments, as when the contractor finances a project by using your home as collateral for a second mortgage.

If the circumstances entitle you to a cooling-off period, the contractor must give you two copies of the Notice of Right of Rescission (see sample, pages 92–93) at the time you sign the contract. The notice must be separate from the contract—not buried in the fine print—and a copy must be given to each owner, because any one owner is entitled to cancel. The notice must identify the transaction, disclose the security interest, inform you of your right to rescind, tell you how to exercise that right, and give you the date the rescission period expires.

Contractors pay attention to this law because if they don't comply, you have the right to rescind for three *years* from the date on the contract—or until you transfer interest or sell the property. Not that you'd want to cancel a job that's already completed, but you might have some leverage to reduce the final payment.

These laws help keep most contractors honest, but they can't keep out all the bad apples. Even if you report violations to the Federal Trade Commission in Washington or one of its ten regional offices, the FTC isn't likely to prosecute a small contractor. Federal enforcement tends to concentrate on major violations or patterns.

State and Local Protection

Fortunately states often have laws modeled after federal laws. State and local agencies are a lot closer to you and a lot more apt to pursue a small contractor who may have violated the law. If you suspect that a contractor you're dealing with is breaking the law, get in touch with your state attorney general's office or local department of consumer affairs.

SAMPLE NOTICE OF RIGHT OF RESCISSION

Notice of Right to Cancel

Your Right to Cancel

You are entering into a transaction that will result in a

___ mortgage
___ lien
___ security interest

in/on your home. You have a legal right under federal law to cancel this transaction, without cost, within three business days from whichever of the following three events occurs last:

1. The date of the transaction, which is _____
2. The date you received your
   truth-in-lending disclosures, which is _____
3. The date you received this notice
   of your right to cancel, which is _____

If you cancel the transaction, the

___ mortgage
___ lien
___ security interest

is also canceled. Within twenty calendar days after we receive your notice, we must take steps necessary to reflect the fact that the

___ mortgage
___ lien
___ security interest

on/in your home has been canceled, and we must return to you any money or property you have given to us or to anyone else in connection with this transaction.

You may keep any money or property we have given you until we have completed the action mentioned above, but you must then offer to return the money or property. If it is impractical or unfair for you to return the property, you must offer its reasonable value. You may offer to return the property at your home or at the location of the property. Money must be returned to the address below. If we do not take possession of the money or property within twenty calendar days of your offer, you may keep it without further obligation.

How To Cancel

If you decide to cancel this transaction, you may do so by notifying us in writing at:

Creditor's (Remodeler's) Name _____

Creditor's (Remodeler's) Business Address _____

_____

You may use any written statement that is signed and dated by you and that states your intention to cancel, and/or you may use this notice by dating and signing it below. Keep one copy of this notice because it contains important information about your rights.

If you cancel by mail or telegram, you must send the notice no later than midnight of (date) _____ or midnight of the third business day following the latest of the three events listed above. If you send or deliver your written notice to cancel some other way, it must be delivered to the address listed above no later than that time.

I hereby cancel my contract.

_____   _____
(Consumer's signature)   (Consumer's signature)

_____ (Date)   _____ (Date)

Reprinted from *What Builders and Remodelers Should Know About Right of Rescission Provisions in the Truth in Lending Act* (Washington, D.C., Consumer Affairs Department. National Association of Home Builders, 1987).

Some states have laws aimed at dishonest contractors. For example, Illinois has a specific Home Repair Fraud Act, strengthened in July 1992. This law makes it a crime to misrepresent the terms of a home repair contract, to deceive people into signing such a contract, to damage property to drum up home repair business, or to change an unconscionable fee. A contractor who preys on disabled people or those over sixty years old may be committing aggravated home repair fraud, a felony punishable by three to seven years in jail and a fine of up to $10,000.

Massachusetts's home improvement law, enacted in 1992, requires all home improvement contractors to register with the state, and requires a written contract with specific elements in it for any home improvement job over $1,000. Violations can trigger fines of up to $5,000 or two years in prison. The statute also establishes an arbitration program for resolving disputes, as well as a guaranty fund to compensate homeowners for unpaid judgments.

The guaranty fund is unusual. In Illinois and many other states, the law provides criminal penalties for errant contractors without providing for restitution for victims. That means defrauded home owners must sue the contractor if they hope to get their money back. But such a lawsuit can be long, costly, and fruitless, because by the time the case comes to trial the contractor may have nothing left to pay.

Localities can also have tough laws against unscrupulous contractors. Putnam County, New York, has a local law that includes such punishments as suspension or revocation of the contractor's license, both criminal and civil penalties, and punitive damages against the unlawful contractor.

To find out the legal protections and enforcement options in your state, contact your state or local consumer protection agency, or the consumer fraud division of the local prosecutor's office.

Beware the Swindler

Despite all the statutes, if you have to rely on the law to get your money back from a shoddy contractor, you'll have to wait a long time. Take matters into your own hands by checking any contractor over carefully in the first place.

Be wary of contractors who:

- claim to work for a government agency. Check it out.

- offer "free" gifts. (What exactly are the gifts? When will you receive them? Can you get a price reduction instead?)

- engage in door-to-door sales or try to get your business by telephone solicitations. Be especially wary if the sales pitch demands that you decide right away to take advantage of prices that won't be available tomorrow. Most reputable contractors have enough business without having to engage in such tactics.

- offer an unsolicited free inspection of your furnace or basement. Ripoff artists use this ruse to get into a home and either fake a problem or damage a sound furnace and good pipes.

- claim your house is dangerous and needs immediate repair—unless *you* already know it does.

- have a company name, address, and telephone number and other credentials that can't be verified. Fly-by-night operators often use a mail drop and an answering service while hunting for victims.

- promise a lower price for allowing your home to be used as a model or to advertise their work. (Has the price really been lowered? What does the "use of your home" entail?)

- engage in bait-and-switch tactics. After luring you with an ad that offers an unbeatable deal on a job, these characters tell you the materials aren't available for that job but they can give you a bargain on another, more expensive, job.

- leave delivery and installation costs out of their estimates.

- offer to give you a rebate or referral fee if any of your friends use the same contractor.

- insist on starting work before you sign a contract.

THREE SCAMS AND HOW TO AVOID THEM

- **The chimney-shaker/furnace-breaker** scams begin with someone at your door purporting to be an inspector, perhaps with an official-sounding agency, who says he must check, say, your furnace. He finds a pretext for getting out of your sight, tampers with the furnace, and informs you that he (or a colleague he recommends) can fix it.

  TIP: Don't let anyone you haven't called or don't expect into your home. Ask to see proper identification. If you're in doubt, ask for the phone number of the person's company and call it (if you get an answering machine, watch out). You can also call the Better Business Bureau and your local or state office of consumer fraud—or any agency the person claims to be with— to ask about the person and his business affiliation. If damage has been done, also call the police to report a crime against your property.

- **"I'm doing work down the street and have some leftovers."** Here, a workman approaches you saying he can save you money if you'll let him do work—perhaps put a new surface

Sam Homeowner, P.I.

After thinking through what you want and what you can afford, ask for recommendations from people who've had similar work done. Talk to building inspectors, bankers, and trade association representatives—people who should know firsthand the work and reputation of contractors in the community.

For a larger job, interview and solicit bids from two or three contractors from your list, making sure they're bidding on exactly the same job to allow accurate comparisons. The lowest bid isn't necessarily the best, because a contractor with a reputation for excellent workmanship and for standing behind the work might be worth more. Even if the job's small enough to warrant only one bid, take time to check out your contractor's reputation and credentials.

on the driveway or add tar to the roof—that you may really need to have done. But, he says, you must do the work now in order to get this bargain price.

TIP: *Resist the temptation to believe this is a stroke of luck. Bargain prices are usually for shoddy work you'll need to have redone. Don't be pressured into agreeing on the spot. Do call and check with the neighbor he says he was working for, or check with the Better Business Bureau, your local consumer fraud office, and the police.*

- **Getting big money by laying claim to your home.** This is a rare but real scam. In 1991, the New Jersey Department of Consumer Affairs, for example, put a stop to dealings of a home-repair contractor and finance company that had de-frauded a number of home owners by overcharging for agreed-to work and then tricking them into signing second mortgages on their homes.

TIP: *Negotiate a good contract and stick to it. Stay away from remodeling projects until you have a good idea of where you can borrow. (Banks and credit unions are generally safer and cheaper than a remodeler might be.)*

Ask contractors about the kinds of jobs they usually do. Get the names of people they've done similar work for recently, and give those people a call. Chances are any such references will be people the contractor knows were happy, so try to go a step or so beyond "He's a great guy" and "No problems at all."

Ask exactly what the contractor did, and how this person found out about him. Jot down any more names that are mentioned, with addresses and phone numbers. Was the client comfortable with the way things were left at the end of a day? at the end of the project? What does the client wish he'd done differently to make the job go even more smoothly? What did the client's spouse (or roommate, neighbors, or children) think about the work and the construction process? What's the next project this person wants to hire the contractor to do (if any)?

If you're satisfied with a contractor's reputation, check his credentials before signing the contract. Ask if he's licensed and bonded. Although not all states require licensing for home contractors, those that do have at the least a record of each contractor's name and address, compliance with insurance laws, and agreement to operate within the law. If it's a corporation, the state has a record of the individual responsible. While some states only require people to register their names and addresses, quite a few require them to have some experience and pass an exam.

Having a state license doesn't mean the contractors will do a good job, but it's some assurance that they've made an effort to comply with the law. You can check with the state Contractors Licensing Board to see if the license is current. Some states will also tell you if there have been complaints against a given contractor and whether they proved to be valid; otherwise you can get that information from your local Better Business Bureau or Office of Consumer Affairs.

Being bonded provides important protections for you, but be aware that the word has two meanings. "Fully insured and bonded" generally means the contractor has insurance coverage to protect his employees' theft, vandalism, or negligence. If you have valuables to consider, ask to see a certificate or letter certifying such a policy.

A performance bond is an insurance company's assurance that the contractor can finish the job as stated in the contract. If he defaults, the insurance company will pay another contractor to complete the work. Contractors have to take out a separate bond for each job, so bonds are usually limited to jobs of $25,000 or more, and contractors pass on the cost to the owner. It's an expensive proposition, up to 10 percent of the contract price for a residential swimming pool. But a contractor who's been approved by a bonding company is a very good risk. You're the one who decides whether to require (and pay for) a bond.

Make sure that the contractor carries workers' compensation insurance, to cover injuries he and his workers might sustain on the job. If he doesn't carry it, you could be responsible for some hefty bills.

Ask if he belongs to a trade association such as the Remodelers Council of the National Association of Home Builders, the

SEVEN THINGS TO REMEMBER
ABOUT ANY CONTRACT

1. *A standard contract is probably far more favorable to the party presenting it—here, the contractor—than to the consumer.*

2. *It is negotiable, and either party may change it by crossing out the contract's language and writing in new provisions—as long as both parties agree by initialing each change.*

3. *It may be preprinted or as casual as a piece of paper or letter of agreement, so long as both home owner and contractor sign it. Sometimes it is simply the proposal that the contractor submits as his bid; when you sign it, it becomes a contract.*

4. *Even a simple word like* consideration *has precise legal meaning that's different from its meaning in everyday language. Don't sign anything until you understand every term (the other party may not be your best source of explanations).*

5. *Sign no contract that has any blank spaces in it. Draw a line or place an x in them.*

6. *Consider signing only in blue ink, to distinguish originals from copies.*

7. *If you're in doubt or if the job is very expensive, the time to talk to your lawyer is before you sign on the dotted line. That's when it's easiest and least expensive to address any problems.*

National Association of the Remodeling Industry, and the National Kitchen and Bath Association. Many associations require a contractor to have been in business a certain length of time, to have passed a credit check, and to meet all legal requirements of their state. It wouldn't hurt to call the association to make sure the contractor's membership is current and inquire about complaints.

Also ask if there is a warranty on his work. On materials? For how long? Make sure any warranty is included in the contract. (Even if there's no specific warranty, most jurisdictions recognize an implied warranty of good workmanship that gives you some protection.) For an additional fee, some contractors offer an extended warranty such as the five-year policies available through the Home Owners Warranty Corporation (HOW).

To see if there are any civil judgments or lawsuits pending against the contractor, check with the local clerk of court. If someone sued the contractor over, say, poor workmanship, take it as a warning. Likewise, you might want to check with the nearest federal bankruptcy court to see whether this contractor has ever filed bankruptcy—a strong indication of financial instability.

As a general rule, don't allow any work to begin until there's a signed contract—one that protects *you*. Oral agreements can be enforced in court, but it's difficult to prove who said what if you don't get it on paper. (If the job is so small that you decide not to bother with a contract, at least ask to see an insurance certificate to make sure the contractor is covered in case one of his subcontractors is injured on your property).

If the contractor gives you a standard contract to sign, take it home and study it carefully at your leisure. You can strike out clauses you think are unreasonable, and have both parties initial the change. Especially if it's a big job and you're uncertain what some of the provisions mean, you may do well to check it with a professional (see box, page 99).

A complete home-improvement contract should address:

- **Preamble.** An introduction that states names, addresses, phone numbers, and date the contract is executed. It should specify whether the contractor's business is a sole proprietorship, partnership, or corporation. (If it's a partnership or corporation, make sure the person who signs is an authorized representative.) The preamble should also state that the remodeler is an independent contractor, not your employee. Otherwise you might be responsible if the builder injures someone. And for another layer of financial accountability, add the contractor's Social Security number.

- **Contract price.** Total dollar amount, including sales tax, to be paid by the home owner for services agreed to in the contract.

- **Starting and completion dates.** No contractor is likely to begin until after your right to rescission (see pages 90–93) has safely passed. Specify an end date, stating exceptions such as weather, strikes, etc. Add a bonus/penalty clause if the date is critical. Specify a daily starting time if that matters to you. Consider interim completion dates for key phases of big jobs.

- **Scope of work.** Contractors may shy away from a clause as broad as "all labor, materials, and services necessary to complete the project." But don't allow them to be so specific in the work listed that anything else becomes an "extra" or a "change order," which may be billed separately.

  See that complete descriptions of agreed-to-products—including brand names and order numbers—are listed. Plans, bids, estimates, and all other documents relating to the project are part of the scope of work; see that copies of these are attached to all copies of the contract before you sign it.

- **Permits, licenses, and zoning.** Specify that the remodeler will obtain all necessary licenses and permits and satisfy all zoning regulations and building codes, and indemnify the homeowner in case he fails to do so.

- **Cleanup policy.** Will the contractor clean up daily? after each project? only at the end? Where is refuse to be placed?

- **Storage.** Specify where materials and equipment will be kept. You are probably liable for damage to materials and equipment from fire or accidents; check your homeowners' policy.

- **Parking.** If it's a problem, arrange for the contractor's vehicle as well as the subcontractor's.

- **Noise.** Some is inevitable and may even provide a safety valve for workers, but place limits on time and volume, according to local laws and neighborhood needs.

- **Theft.** Building materials are often stolen. The contract can make either the contractor or the owner responsible.

- **Damage.** What if the retaining wall collapses when they're digging for the new swimming pool? You'll want the contract to state that the contractor is responsible for damage to your property.

- **Change orders.** Since very few jobs go exactly as planned, the contract should have a provision that enables it to be amended simply and easily. Contracts provide that change orders can be written up, signed by both parties, and attached to the contract as plans change or delays occur. Here's a typical change-order clause:

> Without invalidating this contract, the owner may order changes in the work, including additions, modifications, or deletions. Price and time will be adjusted accordingly. All such changes in the work shall be in writing, and signed by the contractor and owner and attached to this document.

- **Warranties.** Your contract should assure that the materials are new, and that you will receive all warranties from manufacturers for appliances and other materials used on the job.

- **Progress payments.** Contractors don't expect to be paid entirely in advance, but they also don't expect to wait until all work has been done. It's customary to pay one third upon signing a contract to allow the contractor to buy supplies and get started. In smaller projects, two payments may suffice. In larger ones, plan to make payments after completion and approval of major phases of the work.

  In all cases, make your final payment as large as possible, usually at least 10 percent. **DO NOT MAKE FINAL PAYMENT** until all work is completed, inspected, and approved, until subcontractors are paid and any liens canceled, and until all warranties are in the proper hands.

- **Financing contingency.** If your ability to proceed with the project depends on securing outside financing, include a contingency clause stating that the contract is not binding if you're unable to secure the needed funds on acceptable terms.

Ask for a list of subcontractors and suppliers and attach it to the contract with their address, telephone numbers, and Social Security numbers. Though you are not their boss, they probably have a right to place a lien on your home if the contractor does not pay them in full. It's only fair that you know who they are, should legal action become necessary. If you prefer, arrange to pay suppliers and subcontractors directly.

Before the Job Begins

Signed contract in hand, you still should check out a few other details to avoid legal trouble later.

Ask your local department of housing whether you need a building permit. The person who takes out the permit is considered liable for the work, so follow the usual custom of having the architect or contractor obtain it. You as home owner don't want to be responsible if the work doesn't conform to standards or codes, but you need to know which permits are required and make sure they are obtained.

Why bother with a permit? The inspector who checks your house can assure you that the work you're paying for is safe. And if you've followed proper procedures, your house will be free of encumbrances when you want to sell it. In New York, for instance, real estate inspectors can stop property sales when they find disparities between original and remodeled plans of a property. Altered fire-escape routes, often caused by a door or doorway altered without permit and inspection, can be dangerous. And such noncompliance puts the home owner—and buyer—in an expensive bind.

If you live in a condominium or cooperative apartment, or other common-interest property, your rights to renovate and remodel are different from those of owners outright. Check your condominium declaration—or check with your board—to see if your renovation will be permitted. (See chapter 2.)

Local zoning laws may apply if you want to expand your home beyond a certain point. By the same token, such laws may protect your home from encroachment by a neighbor's addition. Call your local zoning board to see whether its regulations affect the work you're planning to do.

Once the Job Begins

The kitchen looks like a war zone and the noise makes an afternoon at the dentist's sound like a treat. Your remodeling project is underway. But in the midst of the confusion, keep a handle on the documents that can help you avoid problems later.

SAMPLE CHANGE ORDER

(Amendment to Contract)

The owner and the contractor agree to the following changes in their contract signed on the _____ day of _____, 19___.

Changes:
   Add water treadmill with 4 HP pump and dual jets to north end of lap lane. Eliminate southeast corner gate.

Price:

   Add $400 to total

   Deduct $120

Total increase $280

Agreed to: _____
                          OWNER

_____CONTRACTOR/DATE

In consultation with your contractor, draw up a schedule of what will be done when and make sure it's followed. If you don't have the wiring inspected before the drywall goes up, the inspector may require you to tear out the drywall.

Contractors report that their biggest problems with home owners come because the owners request additional work along the way, then object when they see the bill. The best way to avoid misunderstanding is with a specific **change order**. This document, signed by both parties and added to the original contract, specifies the additional work to be done, the materials, and any change in the schedule. (See above for a sample.) For a large project, type up and duplicate blank change-order forms to fill out as you need them.

What if someone is hurt on the job? If you were dealing with an independent contractor, his insurance should cover expenses. But if you hired someone down the street to paint your house, someone who doesn't maintain a separate business and who relied on you for tools and supervision, that person is your employee and any injuries are your responsibility. (If someone gets hurt later because, say, the new basement steps weren't nailed down, your insurance company may pay the injured party but then go after the contractor responsible.)

What if you come home from work one day and find that the new picture window that was supposed to face your view of the river has been cut into the wall facing your neighbor's garage?

If you believe there's been a contract violation, first bring the matter to the attention of the contractor. Your first step can be a phone call or conversation. To protect yourself, make a note of the conversation, summarizing your concerns and any agreements, and send it to him. Keep a copy yourself. Step two is asking your lawyer to write a letter stating your concerns and asking for the correction.

If that doesn't work, check to see if your contract specifies alternative dispute resolution (ADR)—that is, mediation or arbitration. That means you and the contractor will have agreed to call in a mutually acceptable third party to resolve the dispute without going to court. If your contract does not specify ADR, your initial letter and the lawyer's letter will provide you with a base for further action with a consumer-protection agency or a lawsuit, possibly in small-claims court.

Either way, your options are to push for **specific performance** of the contract, which means forcing the remodeler to do the work as agreed, or for the remodeler to pay any extra costs you incur by having someone else do it.

Even if the new sun room turns out precisely as you hoped, you may be in big trouble if someone doesn't get paid for making it that way. That's when you might have a lien filed against you. The person filing the lien may ask a court to raise the money by selling your house. Construction liens (also called mechanic's liens) are subordinate to any prior mortgage on your house, so it's a difficult route to payment.

SAMPLE RELEASE OF LIENS

The following contractors and subcontractors have furnished materials and labor for the construction of _____

_____

_____

(describe work completed)

at

(address, lot, block, and square)

and have agreed to release all liens for the above-described work.

Date	Name of Contractor and/or Subcontractor	Signature
____	_____	_____
____	_____	_____
____	_____	_____
____	_____	_____
____	_____	_____

It's possible to add a clause to the contract stating that the contractor agrees to give up his lien rights, but the contractor may not agree to it. And, even with a contractor's waiver, any subcontractor or supplier who isn't paid for his work or materials by your contractor can file a lien against your home.

Unless your job is covered by a performance bond, or your state has some sort of fund to protect home owners from paying twice when the contractor does not pay subcontractors or laborers, your chief protection against a lien is holding back final payment until all work has been completed to your satisfaction and your contractor supplies proof *in writing* that he's paid everyone who worked for him on your job. The **release-of-lien** form included above is useful, since it provides places for all the subcontractors to sign. (This is one reason to have all subcontractors and suppliers named up front in your contract, so you can make sure everyone has signed off on the release-of-lien form.)

In some states, contractors and subcontractors have to notify a home owner if they intend to take out a lien. In others, you only learn about the lien after it's filed at the local recording office. If you find out someone has filed a lien, call your lawyer immediately because the next step might be notice of foreclosure.

CHAPTER SEVEN

■

Love Your Neighbor?

How to Keep Petty Annoyances from Turning into Major Headaches

"PEOPLE JUST WEREN'T MADE TO LIVE in little boxes stacked beside and on top of each other," sighed a police officer investigating a complaint in a suburban condominium complex. The officer shook his head as he slapped a pair of handcuffs on a twenty-eight-year-old aerospace worker. His crime? Playing his stereo too loud.

No joke. After spending a night in jail, the man was scheduled for trial on a misdemeanor charge of excessive noise. Eventually the case was settled, with the offender agreeing to pay a $40 fine and the city agreeing to dismiss the charges. Fed up, the man moved to a house on a large country lot, where he now plays his stereo to his heart's content.

"It is easier to love humanity as a whole than to love one's neighbor," wrote Eric Hoffer in *The New York Times Magazine*. Sad, but true. And modern housing arrangements make it difficult even to *like* one's neighbor, let alone love him.

Take the case of an Illinois home owner who decided to add a second story to his modest ranch home. Then he set his sight on further expansion. Over the years he added on to the house bit by bit until it looked like a 3,300-square-foot Taj Mahal, with plans to expand it to 5,700. For fifteen years his neighbors put up with noisy construction equipment, piles of lumber, stacks of clay roofing tiles and giant sewer pipes, with constant dust and debris. Fed up, the neighbors joined forces with the village to try to get him to complete the project. At this writing the case has festered in court for three years, with no end in sight.

When the people next door carry on their daily activities right under your window, some friction is nearly inevitable. One neighbor likes to hear the birds sing; the other prefers a blasting radio. One wants a view of the mountains; the other wants the privacy of a twenty-foot hedgerow. One thinks the rusty iron fence between the properties is charming; the other thinks it's an eyesore.

If something your neighbor does is bothering you, remember that you'll probably be neighbors for a long time. Resolving the problem amicably may be more important than getting your way completely, because neighborhood feuds are no fun. Case in point: the legendary feud between the Hatfields and McCoys. The two Kentucky families reportedly went to court in 1860 over a disputed hog. Three decades later, the family feud was still raging, even though by then everyone had long forgotten why they were at war.

So talk to your neighbor about the problem and try to work it out. Then try a polite but firm letter. Bringing in the law should be a last resort, not a first one. (For specific steps toward resolving disputes, see the box on page 110.)

In case your efforts to resolve the matter don't work, the law provides several stronger approaches. In many cases, knowing what the law has to say about the situation—and bringing that knowledge to your neighbor's attention—takes care of the problem without further action.

YOUR RIGHTS AS A NEIGHBOR

The problem you face might be addressed in your local government's zoning code, which regulates which activities are permitted in a neighborhood. If you live in a condominium, cooperative or planned subdivision, there might be private regulations and a homeowners' association to back them up. If the offending activity is classified under common law as a nuisance, it might be either a crime or a civil offense under local law. And if the appropriate agency doesn't take action, you could file a lawsuit in

STEP-BY-STEP GUIDE FOR
RESOLVING NEIGHBOR PROBLEMS

STEP 1: **Discuss the problem with the neighbor,** who may not be aware that the late-night parties bother you or that Fifi is digging up your flower bed.

STEP 2: **Warn the neighbor.** Obtain a copy of the applicable local ordinance (look in the **municipal code**, which should be found in your local library or in City Hall, or contact your local council representative). Mail it with a letter of warning alerting your neighbor of a violation of the law. Wait a reasonable time to see if the problem is resolved.

Sample Warning Letter

Dear Neighbor,
　　Just as you enjoy playing your stereo, I enjoy a quiet environment in my home. It is impossible for me to do so when your stereo is played at such a loud volume.
　　Please read the enclosed municipal noise ordinance. You will see that the law requires that you comply and play your stereo only at a reasonable volume.
　　I trust that we can resolve this matter amicably, so that I will not be forced to contact the authorities. Thank you for your anticipated cooperation.

STEP 3: **Suggest mediation.** Try to work out the problem with an impartial third-person mediator to resolve the dispute informally. (The box on page 116 discusses how to find and use a mediator.)

STEP 4: **Contact the authorities.** If all else fails, call the police and/or file a civil lawsuit against the neighbor.

court to stop the activity or in small-claims court for monetary damages.

Let's start with zoning. City or county zoning regulations may limit the height of fences, the use of property for commercial purposes or the decibels of noise allowed at night. In some cases city officials notice a violation and issue a citation, but often it's up to the neighbors to complain.

For instance, a Minneapolis consumer official reports that his office receives numerous complaints about home machine shops that make the neighborhood look like a junkyard and smell like a gas station. Some complainants ask to remain anonymous—including a woman who grew tired of watching her husband tinker with an old junker car in the backyard. "I'm his wife," she said, "but don't tell him I'm the one who called. Just make him get rid of the thing."

If you feel your neighbor may be violating a zoning ordinance, call your city hall or town council and ask if there is a regulation covering your neighbor's act. They may provide you with a copy of the ordinance or direct you to the local library, which usually has such rules on file.

To file a complaint, you may have to contact the city attorney or the controlling agency, such as the local zoning board. Having the city take up the cause for you requires less effort and expense on your part than filing a nuisance suit. However, you won't receive money; your neighbor will either be ordered to comply with the zoning rules, pay a fine to the city, or both.

If you live in a condo, cooperative or planned development, you may be able to take similar measures through the governing board of your complex. Check the bylaws and regulations of your development to see whether there's a rule against the activity in question.

Your homeowners' association can be a powerful ally. After all, if a neighbor's actions are bothering you, they may be equally troublesome to other residents of the development. If your neighbor refuses to comply with your initial requests, consider asking other neighbors if the situation bothers them, too. They may be willing to sign a petition or a joint letter to the homeowners' association, which is more likely to draw the attention of the board than is a complaint from an individual.

The association will investigate the complaint, ask for input from the offending neighbor, then take a vote as to whether official action is warranted. If the board feels your neighbor has violated its governing rules, it will likely begin by issuing a formal warning letter. In extreme cases of noncompliance, homeowners' associations have referred the matter to the city attorney or have filed their own nuisance suits against the offending resident.

Another option is trying to convince the authorities that your neighbor's actions are a **nuisance**, a legal term for unreasonable action by a person that interferes with your enjoyment of your property. It might be noxious gases, annoying wind chimes, foul odors, plaster dust from a neighbor's constant renovations, or even family arguments so loud they bother you at home.

The law of nuisance involves a balancing test, weighing the social value of the activity against the social value of your use and enjoyment of your property. Accordingly the authorities who have to deal with nuisance complaints expect such complaints to be reasonable. You may not like the culinary odors emanating from next door, where your neighbor cooks lots of spicy dishes with garlic and onions. But your distaste for those particular odors is not enough to sustain a nuisance complaint.

If your local ordinances make a nuisance a crime (usually a misdemeanor), the offender might be given a citation to appear in court at a given date, or he might even be arrested, held until he posts bond, and ordered to appear in court. If convicted, he may be fined and/or jailed. If your local ordinances make nuisance a civil violation, he would face civil charges in court. The penalty for a civil violation is a fine.

Whether the alleged nuisance violates a civil or criminal city ordinance, the city carries the burden of prosecuting the case. Your role as the complaining neighbor is limited to testifying if the case goes to trial. Again, any money collected will be in the form of fines paid to the city, not to you.

The other option is to file a nuisance suit yourself. Here you'd bear the expense of bringing the case to trial, including filing fees and legal counsel, but if you won you could collect money damages from the neighbor. A less expensive approach that may be available in your area is to file in small-claims court (see box, pages 114–115). This would cost you less and probably result in a quicker resolution of the matter.

Either way, to prevail against your neighbor in court you'll have to show the following elements:

- The neighbor is doing something that seriously annoys you. It helps to show a copy of a letter you wrote asking the neighbor to stop or modify his behavior.
- The neighbor's actions have reduced your ability to use and enjoy your property.
- The neighbor is responsible for his actions.
- In some states (New Jersey, New Mexico, North Dakota, Oklahoma, and South Dakota), the neighbor's conduct must also be unreasonable or unlawful.
- The annoyance you're suffering would be adequately dealt with by a specific amount of money or an injunction directing the neighbor to do or to refrain from doing something.

WHAT BUGS YOU?

Now let's consider some particular trouble spots and what you can do about them.

Boundary Lines

Disputes about boundary lines are less common than are other neighbor-related problems, in part because of modern surveying techniques. As a rule, boundary lines are set forth in the property description in your deed. Sometimes, though, if the property was originally recorded decades or even centuries ago, that description may be a bit murky.

If you and your neighbor are unsure where the boundaries lie, there are a number of alternatives:

- Spend a few hundred dollars to hire a surveyor.
- File a **quiet title** lawsuit asking a judge to determine where the boundary line is. This is usually more expensive than just hiring a surveyor because you will have to pay court filing fees—with the possibility of also having to pay for a survey if the court so requires.
- Agree with your neighbor that a certain imaginary line or a physical object, such as a fence or a large tree, will serve as the boundary.

SMALL-CLAIMS COURT

If negotiation has failed, your neighbor won't even discuss media-tion, and the local authorities aren't interested, consider small-claims court. You can do it yourself with no lawyers involved. It is less expensive and not subject to the delays of regular court.

The maximum amount you can sue for in small-claims court is usually between $2,000 and $5,000, depending on the state (call the clerk of the court in your county to determine the limits and procedures in your state). Of course you may sue for less than the maximum.

How do you determine the amount to seek? Under the law, you have a right to be "made whole"—that is, for your property to be put back in the condition it was in before encountering problems with your neighbor.

If you have receipts for an item or structure that you had to have repaired, that would be a logical amount to seek. If you haven't made the repairs, you may want to sue for "diminution in value"— the difference between what the property was worth before and af-ter the damage. That can be determined by hiring an appraiser to write a report or by obtaining estimates from two or more rep-utable repair people.

In most states, small-claims court is a fairly simple process. Go to the clerk's office (often located in the municipal court building) and pick up the paperwork to file your claim. If you have questions, an

Each party should sign a quitclaim deed, granting to the other neighbor ownership to any land on the other side of the line.

Be sure to record the deed by filing it in the county records office (often called the "registry of deeds").

Before you erect a fence or other structure on your land, make sure that it is indeed *your* land. If you innocently but mistakenly erect a fence on your neighbor's property, you may be liable for trespassing. She could ask the court for an injunction to make you tear down the fence, as well as for a money payment for any damage you may have caused to her land.

information officer should be there to help you. Ask to see a sample form that has been filled out. There is usually a small fee ($25 or so) to file your claim.

Once you file the form, you will be notified by mail of a hearing date. Before the hearing, be sure to accumulate as much documentation as possible to support your claim. Any recorded evidence supporting your position on the dispute will be helpful; otherwise the judge will be forced to decide exclusively on the basis of what you and your neighbor say in court. Such documentation may include: invoices and canceled checks (showing repair costs to your property), photographs of property damage (before and after if possible), warning letters given to your neighbor (with dates and a signature), and other similar evidence. The hearing may be held in open court or in a private hearing room, depending upon your locality. Usually the judge will listen to both sides and mail you a written decision within a few weeks.

Most small-claims courts can award money only. If you want removal of a fence, tree or noise, you will generally have to file in regular court. The same is true if you want an injunction to get your neighbor to stop doing something that constitutes a nuisance.

But remember, if you are suing for a nuisance or a noise problem, you can sue more than once. As long as the neighbor does not correct the problem, you can sue again and again in small-claims court, receiving monetary compensation each time, until the problem is taken care of.

The same applies in reverse: If your neighbor starts building on a parcel you feel is rightfully your land, notify her immediately. If you allow the construction to continue and wait too long to complain, you may be giving up your right to that strip of land. After many years of uncontested use, courts sometimes grant the party that has used the land a **prescriptive easement** allowing him to continue that use (see chapter 3).

How far over the boundary is enough to complain about? The reasonableness of the circumstances may dictate whether a court will or will not support you. For example, a judge may not be too sympathetic to your request that a neighbor relocate a

MEDIATION

Mediators are trained to listen to both sides in a dispute, identify problems, and suggest compromises and equitable solutions. They provide an impartial and unbiased forum for neighbors to talk.

The key to mediation, unlike a lawsuit, is that it is not an adversary process. No judge makes a decision for either party. The outcome of the dispute is in the hands of both parties. Until both agree, there is no resolution. The parties are more likely to comply with the agreement, since both have had a part in forming it.

You may be able to find dispute resolution services through the Yellow Pages (look under "mediation services" or "arbitration services"). And many bar associations offer nonprofit programs. Many states' Departments of Consumer Affairs have dispute resolution offices also. Consult the state government listings in your telephone directory.

building that is an inch over your property line. However, if that building is flush with your windows and blocking your sunlight and air, the court may come to a different decision.

Noise

In densely populated areas, one of the most common sources of neighborhood tension is noise. Complaints affect even the rich and famous. In 1991, rock star Axl Rose landed in court after a neighbor in his condominium complex accused him of blasting his stereo. The neighbor convinced a court to issue a restraining order to keep the noise to a reasonable level.

Some cities and towns have ordinances limiting noise to a given number of decibels. If the police have a decibel machine, you can ask them to measure the noise your neighbor is creating. This provides useful documentation should you need to proceed against your neighbor in court.

Timing is critical, though. A chain saw buzzing at two in the afternoon is far more reasonable than the same noise at seven on Sunday morning. Accordingly, many municipalities regulate noise levels during certain "quiet times" when most people sleep. These times typically begin between 10 P.M. and midnight and last until 7 or 8 A.M. weekdays; on weekends they often extend to 9 or 10 A.M. But some noises may be unreasonable at *any* time, such as playing an electric guitar so loud that it makes a neighbor's walls shake.

As with any nuisance, start by asking the neighbor to tone down the volume and explain why. Keep a log of the noise—when it occurred, how loud it was, and how it affected your household. If the neighbor doesn't respond even to a letter, consult with your town council about local ordinances that might need enforcement. Consider a lawsuit only as a last resort.

Blighted Property

Unless they're governed by subdivision rules on exterior maintenance, home owners are generally free to choose how their property looks. One exception occurs when a place is so neglected that it becomes a neighborhood eyesore: when the yard is thickly overgrown with weeds or filled with trash, when the property is enclosed by a dilapidated chain-link fence and the windows are all broken. Blighted property decreases the value of surrounding homes and will frequently incur the wrath of neighbors.

If the neighbors refuse your request that they clean up their property to a reasonable standard, you may be able to get the city to make a similar request, provided it has an ordinance declaring blighted property to be a nuisance. If so requested by a citizen— or if a city official observes the nuisance herself—the city may issue repeated notices to the offender. In about 95 percent of the cases, home owners clean up their property after the first notice. About 1 percent of such cases are actually prosecuted in court.

A man in Ventura County, California, found out what can happen when you don't comply with a city's request to clean up your property. Prosecuted by the city on misdemeanor charges over the piles of trash and junk cars on his property, he was jailed twice. While he was in jail, the city undertook the cleanup of his property—then placed a $15,000 lien on his home to recover the cleanup costs.

Illegal Activities

The law may be broad enough to cover "human nuisances" as well, such as drug dealers operating out of a neighborhood home. First, contact the property owner, who may or may not know that her tenants are using the house to traffic in drugs. Some cities require that such tenants be evicted or fine landlords who allow such a nuisance to continue. In some cases, state and federal laws provide for the government to seize property that is being used for illegal financial gain. The threat of forfeiting the house to the government is likely to persuade the home owner to evict the undesirable tenants.

Another approach is for you and your neighbors to pursue a private lawsuit against a neighborhood nuisance. Neighbors can be a powerful, unifying force against a common "enemy." When a pleasant little neighborhood café deteriorated into a notorious drug den, a group of New England neighbors banded together to get the tavern shut down. They jointly hired a lawyer, who persuaded a judge that the establishment constituted a nuisance to the neighborhood. It was promptly shut down, to the collective joy of the neighbors.

Animals

Some neighbors get along like cats and dogs—in some cases, because of cats and dogs.

Consider the situation of two southern California neighbors, one a dog lover and the other a cat lover. Between their yards sat a thick concrete wall. On one side was a litter of normally well-behaved Chinese chow dogs; on the other, two mellow cats.

No problem—until the cats learned how to climb the wall, perch atop it, and glare down at the dogs, just for fun. The dogs took to barking and yapping whenever anything stirred on the other side of the wall.

The entire neighborhood was unhappy. The cat owner blamed the dogs for the noise; the dog owner blamed the cats for teasing the dogs. Even more infuriated was a third neighbor, who worked nights and was trying to sleep when the "dog alarm clock" went off every morning.

The trouble escalated when the dog owner started hurling shoes, balls, and other objects at the cats to chase them off the wall. One unidentified flying object sailing over the wall smacked the cat owner's child on the head. By that point, everyone was threatening to sue everyone else.

The solution? The cat owner suggested a truce: The cats would go out in the mornings and the dogs in the afternoons. By late afternoon, all the animals could go out because the third neighbor would already be at work. The dog owner agreed to stop pitching objects at the cats; the cat owner agreed to pluck the cats off the wall whenever she found them tormenting the dogs. The animal war ended as quickly as it had begun.

When the fur flies between pet owners and their neighbors in Ventura County, California, the confrontation can end up in "animal court," a voluntary program and an alternative to formal court proceedings. There, the county's "poundmaster" presides over about a hundred cases a year, which have included a cat that bit a woman, a rooster that rudely awakened the neighborhood, and a variety of disputes over dogs that bit, barked, or intimidated children.

If your town has no "animal court," it probably has one or more applicable ordinances indexed under "Dogs" or "Animal Control" that can be enforced in regular court. Such laws often limit the number of animals per household, the length of time a dog may bark, or the frequency of barking allowed. Leash laws require that dogs not run at large, and "pooper scooper" laws require owners to clean up after their pets.

If you have a problem with a neighbor's pet, knowing your local laws can add clout to your efforts to resolve that dispute. If polite requests to your neighbor don't work, call your local animal control service, which is likely to be more receptive to your problem than the police or other city officials will be. Unless the animal control authorities consider your complaint unreasonable, they will probably call the offending animal's owner with a warning, followed if the problem persists by a citation. A citation is like a ticket; it requires the offender either to pay a fine or to challenge the citation in court. After being punished in the pocketbook, many people will change their animals' behavior to conform with the law. If they continue to allow their animal to annoy you, they can be fined repeatedly if you continue to complain.

If the problem persists, you may need to bring a civil lawsuit for nuisance to get a court order. The offender is likely to obey, because one who disobeys a court order may find himself in contempt of court, which can mean time in jail or at the bank, withdrawing hefty sums to pay a fine.

For animal problems, call the police only as a last resort. Police are generally not very interested in problem dogs, as they have more important matters to worry about. Bringing the police into the equation also may negate any subsequent attempts to better relations with your neighbor. However, if you have to bring in the police, they might take a variety of steps, including:

- Issuing a citation to your neighbor for violating a municipal code
- Contacting "Animal Control" to confine the animal if it is extremely troublesome or dangerous
- Asking the city attorney to file a criminal complaint against your neighbor, if his action or inaction amounts to a criminal offense

Trees

Trees can cause as much contention between neighbors as can yapping dogs, whether they block people's view, crack a home's foundation, or drop debris on a driveway. Here are the ground rules:

- **Ownership.** A tree whose trunk stands entirely on the land of one person belongs to that person. If the trunk stands partly on the land of two or more people, it usually belongs to all the property owners.
- **Damage.** Someone who cuts down, removes, or harms a tree without permission owes the tree's owner money for compensation for the harm done.
- **Trimming.** Dangerous limbs falling onto another's property can cause real problems. You may trim the branches of a neighbor's tree that hang over your property, with certain restrictions:
  You may trim up to the boundary line only.

You need permission to enter the tree owner's property (unless the tree threatens "imminent and grave harm" to you or your property).

You may not cut down the entire tree.

You may not destroy the tree by trimming it.

Are you liable for the encroachment of your trees or shrubbery on a neighbor's property? The law varies from state to state, but in general it depends largely on the extent of damage done. It's best to avoid a confrontation—legal or otherwise.

For instance, two California neighbors who lived on tightly adjoining lots in a small housing tract resolved a dispute over a tree that overhung both of their driveways. Neighbor One, a meticulous man, was dismayed when Neighbor Two's tree began to shed a sticky substance all over his new car. Neighbor One insisted that offending limbs be cut down, but Neighbor Two's gardener balked.

The solution? Both neighbors agreed to use the same gardener, and jointly instructed him in how the tree should be maintained on a regular basis.

If your neighbor complains about the encroachment of your leaves or vines, offer to remove them. Roots are a more serious (and potentially costly) problem. You will save money in the long run by hiring a landscaper or tree surgeon to take whatever steps are necessary to prevent root damage to your neighbor's home or wall.

It's always best to notify the tree owner before starting any trimming, pruning, or cutting. If the owner objects to the trimming, offer reassurance that the job will be done professionally and responsibly, within the mutual rights of both parties involved.

Fruit-bearing trees that overhang a neighbor's property pose a more tasty dilemma. When apples drop onto the neighbor's property, is the fruit considered manna from heaven? According to a long-standing common law doctrine, no. The fruit belongs to the owner of the tree—and so it has been since the 1800s, when a man named Hale scooped up twenty bushels of pears from the orchard trees of his neighbor. A court ordered Mr. Hale to return his booty to the orchard owner, even though Hale had been standing on his own land when he plucked the fruit.

What if your neighbor's fruit is a problem for you? If rotting fruit habitually falls from a neighbor's tree into your yard, notify him. Ask him to clean the fruit from your yard and to trim the tree to avoid such droppings in the future. If he ignores your request or refuses to comply, your neighbor may be liable for any damages the errant fruit causes to your grass or garden. (The same thing goes for the fruit of a neighboring tree that may cause physical injury to *you*, such as a coconut that falls from a high tree and smacks you on the head.)

Trees are not strictly private property like barbecue grills. In some instances, neither the tree owner nor the neighbor has unlimited control over the fate of a tree. One subdivision overlooking scenic Farmington Valley in Simsbury, Connecticut, has a restrictive covenant in its deeds bearing homage to trees: Home owners cannot cut them down, even on their own land. They can, however, trim diseased limbs or branches that block their view of the valley below.

Subdivision rules such as this are designed to restrict the use of each lot in a tract for the benefit of all who reside there. One lot owner can enforce the restriction against another. If you are considering buying property in a subdivision, ask about any such restrictions in the general building plan.

Views

Residents of certain parts of the country, particularly on waterways, are protective of the scenic view from their property. If view is important to you or to the value of the property you are considering buying, be sure to investigate your legal rights to protect that view before closing the deal.

What can you do if you wake up one morning and find a new fence on your neighbor's land blocking your view of Big Sur? That depends in part on where you live. Generally there is no absolute right to a view, air, or light, unless granted in writing by a law or subdivision rule. Such provisions are more common in coastal areas or other scenic-view locations.

The best way to protect a view is to purchase an easement from your neighbor, guaranteeing that no obstruction of your view will be built on the land described in the easement. (See the section on easements in chapter 1.) You may cringe at the thought of paying for a view that is already there, but in the long run it is likely to be less costly—and more scenic—to buy an easement now than to bring a lawsuit in the future.

That's why a Los Angeles Supreme Court judge ordered the rock star Madonna to trim her driveway hedges to eight feet in height and to trim a pine tree down to her roof level—and to pay the legal fees of the neighbor who brought the lawsuit against her. The neighbor contended that the untrimmed foliage blocked his Hollywood Hills view of the city lights below and reduced the value of his property. He was able to prevail because he had a longstanding written agreement with her regarding his view, so he simply went to court to enforce that contract.

Unless you live in a community that has a view ordinance, you are unlikely to get relief in the courts without such a contract. But even given a view ordinance, the mayor won't necessarily jump in and order your neighbor to tear down the obstruction. If the city does not feel your complaint has merit, you will have to initiate a lawsuit and wait until your day in court to request an order requiring your neighbor to restore your view. Depending upon the backlog in your local courts, that wait could be months. And of course your neighbor might appeal the decision, causing another lengthy delay.

In the interim, get used to looking at fence posts instead of whitewater. In the interests of time and sanity, it may be advisable to forego the legal wrangling and negotiate with your neighbor. If your city does not have a view ordinance, you can still ask a court to have the offending fence or tree removed if you can show that by erecting or planting it, your neighbor was "deliberately and maliciously" trying to block your view. This would fall under the category of **spite fences** (see below).

Fences

The word *fence* is not limited to the picket or stockade-type barrier you may imagine. Fence ordinances generally cover anything that serves as an enclosure or partition, including trees or hedges. Keep in mind that a living "fence" that started out as a legal four-foot-high hedge may grow into an unpermitted twelve-foot-high wall. Many zoning regulations restrict the height of fences, whether they are made of cut timber or living trees.

Consider the plight of a Huntington Beach, California, family whose backyard was bordered by towering beautiful Italian cypress trees, ranging from twenty to thirty feet in height. Their neighbors complained to the city, which served the family with a notice to cut all the trees down to the required six-foot height limit. A tree expert affirmed that lopping off the trees would kill them, certainly not what the neighbors wanted. The city allowed the existing trees to be "grandfathered" in under a use permit.

A fence that sits directly on the property line of two neighbors is known as a **boundary fence**. The legal rights and responsibilities depend on a number of factors, including who "uses" the fence.

As a general rule, boundary fences are somewhat like trees that straddle a property line—they belong to *both* property owners. That means both neighbors are responsible for the upkeep of the fence and neither may remove or alter the fence without the other's permission.

Of course, the owners are free to agree otherwise. One may wish to "buy" the fence from the other and have it recorded in his deed for posterity. Or one neighbor may be willing to give up his "share" of the fence if the other agrees to pay for the maintenance.

If you live in a historic part of the country, beware of obscure laws that may still be on the books. In Maryland, a Howard County landowner was subjected to an anachronistic county law that not only required him to share the cost of a fence on the property line with his neighbor, but required the fence to be "hog-tight"—low enough so that a hog could not squeeze under it. And no, neither of the neighbors had any hogs on his property. (At last report, county officials were working to repeal the law.)

A **spite fence** is one that is excessively high, has no reasonable use to your neighbor, and was clearly constructed to annoy you. For example, suppose you live atop a canyon view and you've been feuding with your neighbors, who live farther down the slope. The neighbors suddenly erect a twenty-foot-high stockade fence near the property line. You can sue them under the doctrine of private nuisance. The case may be difficult to win, however, because most fences or other structures have some arguable utility to the owner. Your neighbors may be able to demonstrate a reasonable need for such a high fence, such as extra privacy concerns.

If you win, your remedies, depending on the law of the state in which you reside, may include an injunction to have the fence removed (or at least lowered to a less offensive height) or compensatory damages (a money payment to you). Factors the court will consider in determining the appropriate amount of compensation include the diminished value of your property and any annoyance caused by the erection and maintenance of the fence. However, you cannot recover for "hurt feelings" or embarrassment due to the fence.

Most spite fences spring from a history of bad feelings in the neighborhood, which deteriorate into anger and spite. That's why it pays to be neighborly in the first place. Cooperating with your neighbors can make life easier for everyone.

■

CHAPTER EIGHT

Money, Money, Money!

The Financial Side of Home Ownership

M ONEY CAN'T BUY HAPPINESS, but it can buy a really nice place to live. You can bet that the millions of Americans now renting apartments would be quick to buy their own place if only they had the money. As a home owner, you've cleared that hurdle already. Feels good, doesn't it?

But there's more to the financial side of home ownership than saving up enough for a down payment and earning enough to make the mortgage payments. You'll want to keep an eye on your lender or mortgage service company to make sure you're not the victim of costly accounting errors. You'll want to make sure your family would have enough money to pay the mortgage if something happened to you. When interest rates drop, you'll want to know how to decide whether to refinance. If you run into financial problems, you'll want to know your legal rights and responsibilities—and what your lender can do to protect its interest. And when the glorious day arrives when you have enough money, you'll want to know how and when to pay off your mortgage so you'll own that home free and clear.

So here's a chapter dedicated to money, a poor master that is nonetheless a good servant.

MANAGING YOUR MORTGAGE

When you closed on your home, chances are your lender or mortgage service company gave you a fat book of payment coupons to tear off and include with each monthly payment. The coupons and stubs declare the amount you owe each month so it's easy to keep track.

Mortgage payments are almost universally due on the first of each month. Many lenders allow a two-week grace period, then charge a late fee on payments received after the fifteenth. But don't get in the habit of sending your payments late; if you're persistently delinquent, your lender may be entitled to accelerate the loan.

On the other hand, if all you do is dutifully pay what you're told, you might be paying more than you have to. In some cases, a whole lot more. Be vigilant; keep tabs on your monthly statements. Here are some areas to watch.

Change in Servicers

When you get a new or refinanced mortgage, don't be surprised if your lender promptly sells the mortgage to a mortgage service company, because many banks don't keep residential mortgages in their portfolios. It has nothing to do with your payment history or the quality of your loan, but these banks don't consider mortgage servicing to be cost effective. If your loan is sold, you'll get a welcome letter with instructions to send your payment to a different lender, and (perhaps later) a new coupon book. (If the coupon book doesn't arrive before you have to send the next month's payment, write your loan number on the check and send it on time.)

What if you have an **escrow account**, in which your lender sets aside part of payment to cover your taxes and insurance premiums? It's your old servicer's responsibility to inform your insurance company and taxing authority of the switch. You might want to make a few calls, though, to make sure the bills are sent to the new servicer. Ditto for mortgage life and disability policies.

If your mortgage is paid through an automatic draft or electronic funds transfer, it's up to you to cancel that arrangement and fill out new forms to set up a new one with the new servicer. This takes time; keep tabs on the switch and be prepared to send a check yourself to make sure you don't miss a payment date. If you accidentally send a payment to the old servicer, chances are it'll be forwarded, but in case of a merger or takeover the old servicer may not exist and your payment could take the slow route through return mail. So be sure to follow the instructions in your welcome letter.

Don't switch where you send your payments, though, until you've gotten word from your original lender confirming that the loan has indeed been sold to that company. There's a scam for every type of transaction, and mortgage servicing is no exception. Some home owners have gotten phony letters informing them that their mortgages have been sold and directing them to send their payments to a new address—where they go into the pocket of a resourceful scam artist. If you haven't heard about a transfer from your original lender, call to see whether it's legitimate.

Even a legitimate switch in loan servicers can spell trouble. You might send your payment on time to the new place, but get hit with a late fee because the new loan servicer doesn't have its computer geared up for recording payments on its new portfolio of mortgages. Or the new servicer might recalculate your escrow and decide you owe more than you think—due immediately.

Since 1990, federal law has required loan originators to give borrowers fifteen days notice if their loan is to be transferred. The letter is supposed to identify a toll-free or collect number to call with questions. If a borrower sends a payment to the old servicer, the new one can't charge a late fee within six days of the transfer. And if you contact the loan servicer with a payment dispute, the company can't report your overdue payment to a credit reporting company for sixty days.

Although this law is designed to protect consumers, it hasn't stopped all transfer-related problems. Even with a clear-cut error, it's often very difficult to get the new lender to acknowledge the problem and get it straightened out. If you discover an error and you're getting nowhere with the company, contact your state office of savings and residential finance for consumer assistance.

Escrow Charges

Your mortgage lender has an interest in making sure your property is adequately insured and that your property taxes are paid. Accordingly the law allows lenders to require you to pay money into an escrow account, from which the lender pays the insurance premium and tax assessment (your tax and insurance bills go directly to the lender). It's sort of like enforced budgeting, to make sure you don't come up short when it's time to pay.

Veterans Administration (VA), Federal Housing Administration (FHA) and private mortgage insurance (PMI) loans always require escrow accounts for insurance premiums and property taxes. Conventional home loans may or may not, but many lenders routinely include them in the conditions for making the loan. Whether or not you have to escrow your payments may be negotiable, but the time to negotiate is at the outset. Lenders like having the use of that money until the payments are due.

In most states, lenders don't have to pay interest on escrow accounts, so it's free money for them. In California, Connecticut, Iowa, Maine, Maryland, Massachusetts, Minnesota, New Hampshire, New York, Oregon, Rhode Island, Utah, Vermont, and Wisconsin, state law requires lenders to pay interest. Federally chartered banks, though, are exempt.

The question is how much money mortgage holders have to put into escrow. It's a bit tricky to monitor because money is going in and out of your escrow account as your mortgage payments come in and the lender makes your insurance and tax payments. Federal law limits escrow accounts to the amount needed to pay two months' worth of each borrower's obligations. That is, if the lender is to cover $1,200 in tax payments and insurance premiums, that's $100 per month, so the lender could collect enough of your money into escrow to make the payments while maintaining a $200 cushion in case of unexpected increases. At some time every year, the account should be down to that $200 figure.

This is such a complex process that a significant number of escrow accounts contain either too much or too little of the borrower's money. A recent HUD study indicated that more than 10 percent of American home mortgage escrow accounts are illegally high, but nearly 25 percent aren't high enough to cover the lender's expenses. In those cases, lenders essentially advance home owners the money to make the required payments. So your lender's escrow practices might actually be in your favor.

In many cases, though, home owners are paying more into escrow than they need to. Loan servicing companies often change the way they figure the escrow on newly purchased loans, resulting in sudden major increases.

Your lender is required to send you a summary of your escrow account activity once a year. Make sure your payments are being made on time and check how much you're paying in and how much is going out. If your escrow account or your monthly payments seem too high, ask for an explanation. Lenders are allowed to keep no more than two months' payments (plus fifty dollars) in your account. If you find a mistake, you can demand a refund. New escrow rules from the Department of Housing and Urban Development require lenders to refund excess money. (See box, opposite, for information on mortgage monitoring companies.)

Adjustable Mortgage Rate Errors

If you have an adjustable rate mortgage (ARM), your interest rate changes periodically, depending on what's happened to the prime rate. Because your lender didn't have to guarantee a set rate for fifteen or thirty years, you probably started with a lower interest rate than did people with fixed-rate mortgages—a good deal if you may not keep the house more than a few years anyway.

Lenders use several formulas for determining what the rate will be each period, such as two points over a particular Federal Home Loan Bank District's cost of funds, or one point over the yearly average rate for one-year Treasury bills. Check your disclosure statement to see what formula applies in your case. If your lender uses a different formula than agreed, the error can add up over the years to hundreds or even thousands of dollars.

Likewise, if you prepay principal, it's important to make sure the prepayments are actually applied to principal. Otherwise, you may end up paying more than you owe.

Ferreting out such errors is tricky business, because you need to know your way around amortization tables to see what's going on. As with escrow errors, an accountant or a mortgage monitoring company (see box on page 131) could check your statements for you and see if there's an error in the lender's favor. In nearly half the cases, however, errors are in the borrower's favor.

Private Mortgage Insurance

Private mortgage insurance (PMI) is different from mortgage life insurance, which pays off your mortgage if you die (see below), and from homeowners' insurance, designed to replace your home and possessions in case of fire, theft, etc. (see chapter 4). Lenders often insist on PMI if you have a low down payment, such as only 5 percent, on an original loan. The idea is to protect the lender's interest; if you default on the loan, the insurer will cover the lender's losses. As home prices have outpaced buyers' incomes, the number of conventional mortgages carrying PMI has grown to nearly 30 percent.

The problem is that PMI, which costs about 0.3 percent of the loan per year, doesn't self-destruct when it's no longer needed. When you've built enough equity in your home, your lender wouldn't need PMI anymore to protect its interest because it could go after your equity. But nothing in the PMI policy says when it can be dropped, and it doesn't disappear without your taking some initiative. Many home owners pay for PMI year after year when they no longer have to.

Some lenders and investors require PMI for the entire term of the loan. That's a matter to negotiate if you refinance; make sure you can drop it when you reach a certain level of equity. Typically, the threshold is 20 percent equity. But few lenders will allow you to drop it if you've missed a payment; even a few late payments can make it tough to remove.

If you live in an area where property values are rising and you've been diligent about your payments, it shouldn't be a problem to negotiate removal of PMI once you've reached 20 percent equity. Contact your lender or mortgage servicing company and explain why you shouldn't have to pay it anymore. There's no set rule; determinations are made on a case-by-case basis.

You might be able to show that your home's value has increased enough that the remaining mortgage is less than 80 percent of the current appraised value. For that argument you might need a new appraisal, which could cost you around $400. But if you can show what similar homes in the neighborhood have sold for recently, you may be able to convince your lender without one.

HOT DEALS

The pitch from your banker arrived in the mail yesterday, and it looks like a really good deal. Maybe it's a mortgage life insurance policy designed to pay off your mortgage balance if, heaven forbid, you should die suddenly and your loved ones couldn't make payments on the house. Maybe it's a home-equity loan that would consolidate all your bills into one lower, monthly, tax-deductible payment. Or maybe it's a good rate on a second mortgage that could give you the money you need to build that addition. What a deal! Should you go for it?

Think twice. Lenders are quick to offer financial plans to protect or expand your mortgage, promising to help you cope with your financial problems, real or imagined. But while some of these are merely unnecessary, others can draw you deeper into debt than you already are—and the price you'll pay for slipping up is your house. Talk it over with a savvy adviser you trust—and not the one who's trying to sell you on the deal.

Here are some of the mortgage-related deals you may be offered, with some thoughts on what they can and can't do for you.

Mortgage Life Insurance

Although you can buy mortgage life insurance at any time, it's a standard extra offered by banks before closing. "You want this, don't you, to make sure your family can meet the mortgage payments if you die?" Basically, it's a special kind of term insurance, which either pays off the mortgage or covers the monthly payments if the insured dies. Two home owners can typically be insured for roughly half again the premium, so the policy pays if either one dies. A surviving spouse who receives a lump-sum benefit can invest the money and use the interest to make mortgage payments.

As with any form of life insurance, the premium depends on your age. If you're under thirty-five it might cost less than $10 per month, compared to, say, $135 per month if you're sixty-five. The premium on an existing policy doesn't necessarily increase, though, as you get older. To cover the premiums, your lender increases your monthly mortgage payments.

One variation is disability insurance, a separate policy that would cover your mortgage payment for, say, up to two years if you were disabled. Since temporary disability is more likely then premature death, premiums might run $20 per month for a monthly benefit of $700. Again, the payments would be added to your monthly mortgage payments.

Although it's a good idea for families to buy some kind of life and disability insurance to protect their home, you can probably get a better deal than the policies offered on a take-it-or-leave-it basis by your lender. One reason is that you have no opportunity to compare costs. Term insurance premiums and benefits vary quite a bit from one company to the next, and you're better off shopping around.

Although mortgage life insurance is better than no life insurance at all, its premiums are the highest per thousand dollars of coverage of any form of life insurance. Any kind of life insurance could be used in part to pay the mortgage. In fact, enough straight term insurance to cover expected needs is probably a better idea because the benefit level remains constant. The benefit paid by mortgage life insurance decreases as you pay down the mortgage, because it only covers the amount still owed. An equal amount of level term insurance doesn't cost much more.

Be especially skeptical of mortgage life insurance if you've been paying on your mortgage for quite a few years. By that time, your debt has decreased so much that you could be paying hundreds of dollars per year to cover a small balance. Chances are you'd be well advised to cancel the policy.

Since mortgage life insurance is designed to help a homeowner's spouse and children, it makes no sense at all if you're single. Not unless you want your parents or whoever inherits your estate to inherit your house debt-free.

Second Mortgages and Home-Equity Loans

A home-equity loan sounds appealing because it promises to free up the equity you've built in your home—the difference between what your home is worth and what you owe on it. Maybe you want to redo the kitchen but need extra cash to do it. Maybe you'd like to consolidate all your bills by borrowing enough on your home's equity to pay them all off, leaving you with a single, lower monthly payment. Either way, the interest is tax deductible. In pitch letters from the bank, it sounds pretty good.

Really, though, a home-equity loan is just a glorified second mortgage. A typical lender will loan you 75 or 80 percent of your home's appraised value, less what you owe on it. Interest rates are higher than for first mortgages because of greater risk for the lender. You're putting your home up as collateral on the loan; if you can't pay it back (while keeping up with your regular mortgage payments), the lender has a right to foreclosure. So be sure you know what you're getting into.

These loans take two basic forms. A standard installment-type second mortgage, also called a home-improvement loan, is for a given amount of money at a fixed rate of interest for a stated term: say, $10,000 at 9 percent for fifteen years. You get the money in a lump sum along with a second coupon book. You pay a set amount per month over and above the payments you make on your first mortgage. A home-equity line of credit is flexible both in what you borrow and how much interest you have to pay. Based on your equity, the lender gives you a set of checks to use as you need the money, up to a certain credit limit. When you draw on your credit line you activate an adjustable interest rate, typically one percentage point above the prime rate (if interest rates start climbing, you may be in for more debt than you expected). As with a credit-card account, you have to make a minimum monthly payment, such as 2 percent of the balance or a stated flat sum. But you're probably only paying interest; the principal is due in a balloon payment (a huge payment due at the end of the term, to make up for the very low monthly payments) when the line of credit expires.

Both home-equity lines of credit and standard second mortgages involve $100 to $400 in closing costs, including a title search, appraisal, and recording fee. Some lenders also charge points, say 1 percent of the loan amount in extra interest up front.

If you decide to go for this extra cash, which form you choose will depend on your needs. If you need a a set amount all at once, say to add a room to your house, a fixed-rate second mortgage can reduce the temptation to use the money (and run up your debt) for other purposes. If you're remodeling in stages or putting a child through college, the flexibility of a home-equity line of credit might be better. But think long and hard before you commit yourself to either type. Remember, you're betting your house on your ability to pay back the money.

Home-equity loans packaged as bill-consolidation loans are especially tempting if you've run up a lot of bills, because the interest rates are generally lower than for credit cards or auto loans. You can indeed lower your monthly payment, but in most cases you're agreeing to a longer payback term than you had before. A car that would have taken only three or four years to pay off will now take ten or fifteen. If you have $20,000 of credit card debt at 18 percent, you can replace it with a $20,000, ten-year home-equity loan at 12 percent. By the time you're done, though, you'll have paid $40,000 in principal and interest.

Worse, if you're the kind of person who runs up bills and has trouble paying them, what if you need to buy a new car before you pay off that second mortgage? Many people who take out a bill-consolidation loan to pay off their accounts find they have credit available again—and can't resist the temptation to use it. But if you get into yet another installment credit deal, you'll be in worse shape than you were before: a mortgage, a second mortgage, and another pile of bills.

You could incorporate the new bills into a renewed consolidation loan with a bigger monthly payment, but that would free up more credit and make it possible to get even deeper into debt. When it's finally time to face the music, you'd realize that the bill consolidation loans converted ordinary, unsecured credit into fully secured mortgage debt. That means your lender has a right to foreclose on your house and have it sold to pay it all off.

REFINANCING

A few years ago, many home owners refinanced their mortgages. If they bought their homes back when annual interest rates hovered around 11 and 12 percent, they saved a great deal of money over the term of the mortgage by going through the hassle of refinancing. Many were able to switch from a thirty-year mortgage to a fifteen-year mortgage, so they could pay off their loan in half the time with roughly the same monthly payments.

Although some might claim otherwise, no one really knows where interest rates are heading. If they climb, you'll be glad to have refinanced at a low rate. If they drop, you can refinance again in a year or two. Even if you refinanced just last year, it may be worth your while to do it again if interest rates have fallen a point or two since then.

Especially if your loan is fairly recent, you may be able to go back to the lender who wrote your original mortgage and sign a few papers. Savings and loans and small town banks, which often keep mortgage loans in their portfolios, are often willing to modify a recent existing loan rather than risk losing your business. Instead of refinancing, which means paying off the loan and replacing it with a new one, you cut a deal with the lender to bring the existing loan in line with the market. The new rate might be slightly higher than what you could get if you refinanced, but the costs could be significantly lower because the lender knows your payment history. For loans originated within the past few years, some lenders require only a one-page loan modification form and a fee of, say, $750. Ask your lender if a loan modification is feasible in your case.

Likewise, if you hold a VA or FHA mortgage you can probably renegotiate your loan rather than refinance it. Both agencies offer a process they call "streamlining," designed to provide more favorable financing for people who've made their payments on time and who don't want to increase the size of their loan. After all, home owners with the wherewithal to make their existing mortgage payments would be perfectly capable of making lower ones. Ask your lender about streamlining your loan.

Otherwise, refinancing can be a major hassle because many banks routinely bundle up their mortgages and sell them to a mortgage service company, which collects mortgage payments from the home owners and makes sure insurance premiums and property taxes are paid. If the bank keeps any papers on the loan at all, they're outdated. So if you go back to your original lender to refinance, it may be essentially the same as starting over—with application fee, survey, title insurance, points, and closing costs.

Should You Refinance?

Refinancing shouldn't be a big deal, but it usually is. The process is surprisingly complicated, takes a good two months, and can cost nearly as much as getting a new loan.

Is it worth the effort? That depends on your circumstances. The old rule was to do it if you could lower your interest rate by at least two percentage points, because it would take that much savings to cover the fees associated with refinancing. In today's competitive market, though, many lenders may offer to eliminate application fees, points, or other loan fees, which can make refinancing less expensive for you.

Experts now advise home owners to work from how long they expect to own the home. Ask a lender you're considering what the closing costs and monthly payments would be for refinancing your loan. Divide the closing costs by the amount you'd save each month. That will give you the number of months you'd need to keep the home to recover the cost of refinancing.

Suppose you have a $100,000 thirty-year, fixed-rate mortgage at 9.5 percent, which requires a monthly payment of $840.86 for principal and interest. You replace it with a similar mortgage at 7.8 percent, requiring monthly payments of $719.88. That's a monthly savings of $120.98. Now suppose you have to pay three closing points, or $3,000, plus $250 for an appraisal fee and $350 for title insurance, for a total closing cost of $3,600. Divide that number by $120.98 and you get just under 30, the number of months of mortgage savings it would take to recover that cost. So you'd have to own your home for two and a half years before refinancing would really start to pay off. But if you keep it for twelve years, you'll save nearly $14,500.

Not everyone can refinance, though. If you're one of the unfortunates whose property value has plummeted in recent years, you may have trouble finding a bank willing to refinance. That's because the amount remaining on your loan is more than your home is now worth, and mortgage lenders are bound by strict state and federal guidelines spelling out the percentage of current value they can lend. You can't get a new loan without having a certain amount of equity in the home. If possible, consider cashing in a chunk of your savings and paying down the existing loan far enough to permit refinancing.

Generally speaking, you can refinance if your home is worth 10 percent more than the loan amount. If you buy private mortgage insurance (PMI), you can get away with 5 percent. (See above, under "Managing Your Mortgage," for more on PMI).

Even if you can refinance and it pencils out to significant monthly savings, be aware that starting over on your loan means you'll end up paying more in interest than you would otherwise—especially if you've been paying on your loan for quite a few years. Lenders allocate your month's payment first to pay whatever interest you owe for that month, then apply whatever's left to principal. Out of an initial payment of $1,800, maybe only $10 goes toward the principal of the loan; the rest is interest. It's several years before you start making significant payments toward the principal; at about year twelve of a thirty-year mortgage, payments to principal and interest are roughly equal. Check your most recent statement to see how much of your latest payment went to principal and how much went to interest.

If you're to the point where you're making significant inroads on the principal, starting over with a new loan means you'll be back to paying almost all interest. Many people never intend to stay in a house long enough to pay off their mortgage, but if you think you will, it might make more sense to build equity even faster by prepaying some of your principal. Of course, that would mean paying more each month (see below for more on prepaying).

Fixed Rate or Adjustable?

As with your original mortgage, if you refinance you'll have to choose between a fixed rate or an adjustable-rate mortgage (often called ARM). Instead of having a set interest rate over the term of the loan, an ARM is adjusted periodically within a set range. Your loan documents might specify adjusting the rate every six months, every year, or every three years. Often the standard is one percentage point over the prime rate set by the U.S. Treasury. It's possible to switch from one form to the other for a modest fee.

Do you plan to stay in your home for ten years or more? In that case, your best bet is probably the certainty of a fixed-rate mortgage even if the initial rate of interest is a bit higher. Since the cost of money could be much higher a few years down the line, lenders charge more for fixed-rate mortgages. But if you see rates dropping, you can always refinance again in a couple of years.

If you're only planning to keep the house another two or three years before trading up or moving elsewhere, you might as well get the lowest rate available—an ARM. These are often discounted the first year to make them especially attractive, but watch out for "sucker" adjustables that skyrocket after the first

SHOPPING FOR A REFINANCING DEAL

If you're thinking about refinancing, take time to shop around. These days lenders are scrambling for a chunk of the refinancing market, sending out promotions designed to grab your attention by offering low interest rates and minimal closing costs. Competition has led to a wide range of options, so don't jump on the first offer that comes your way. Check with several mortgage bankers, savings and loans, and other lending institutions.

If you're considering a fixed-rate mortgage, be sure that you're comparing annual percentage rate (APR), which factors in points (interest paid up front), rather than the "simple" interest rate, which doesn't include all the costs of closing.

If you're looking at an adjustable-rate mortgage (ARM), the Federal Trade Commission recommends comparing:

- *initial interest rates*
- *the "cap," which is how much the rate can increase over the life of the loan*
- *how often the interest rate can change*
- *how much and how often the monthly payments and term of the loan can change*

few months. Even with a normal ARM, be aware that interest rates may surge unexpectedly, leaving you with a higher monthly payment than you'd planned on. That's bad news if you're barely making it as it is, or if you or your spouse is unable to work for awhile.

If you already have an adjustable-rate mortgage and interest rates have dropped considerably since the last adjustment, you may be able to lower your interest by asking your lender to make the adjustment earlier than scheduled. Many are willing to make this modification for a small fee.

You might be offered a "balloon note," which is amortized like a thirty-year mortgage but has to be paid off with a huge final payment in five or ten years. The problem is that you don't know what your circumstances will be at that time; you may be

- what index is used to determine rate changes
- what "margin" is used (how much more a lender can add to the adjusted interest rate)
- any "balloon" payments (a large payment due at the end of the term, to make up for low monthly payments)
- the limits on "negative amortization" (loss of equity when payments are so low that they don't fully cover the interest rate charges, so you owe more at the end of the year than you did at the start)

If you find a promising deal, don't rely on it without having the lender give you a written "lock-in" (also called a "rate lock" or "rate commitment"). This is a guarantee that the lender will hold a particular interest rate and number of points for you for a specified period while your loan application is being processed. Otherwise, things could change by closing time. Some lenders charge an application fee of $200 to $500 to lock in rates, which may not be refundable if you don't close for some reason. Others don't. Ask if any application fee can be applied to other charges if the loan goes through, and refunded if it doesn't.

disabled or unable to qualify for refinancing. The only balloon note to accept is one that guarantees refinancing at the rate then current.

Pinning It Down

Be sure to shop at several banks, thrifts, and mortgage companies to see what deals are available. A mortgage broker can help you shop around, but get recommendations from people you trust before engaging one. (For more on what to compare, see box, above.)

Before settling on a refinancing deal, you might want to engage a lawyer to look out for your interests and make sure everything is filed properly. Some states require using lawyers; otherwise, hiring a lawyer is a matter of personal preference.

Ask plenty of questions and make sure you get straight answers. Beware of "bait and switch" tactics, where a mortgage broker gets your business with the promise of an especially good deal then claims he couldn't get it past the lender. Ask for a written list of all fees, then check the list at closing to make sure no extra charges have been slipped in. Also check all the numbers twice at closing to make sure, for instance, that your latest mortgage payment has been credited.

If your old lender has some of your money in escrow for property taxes and insurance (see pages 128–131), don't expect to get that money back right away. Lenders often keep escrow funds up to sixty days to cover outstanding tax or insurance bills. When you do get the refund, make sure your premium or taxes weren't paid by both lenders.

FINANCIAL PROBLEMS

When you applied for a mortgage to buy your home, the lender made sure you'd be able to manage the payments on the income you had then. But what if you or your spouse is laid off, your income plummets, and you can't make your payments?

Your mortgage documents allow your lender to take steps to recover the money you owe. In some states, that might be if you're even a few days late. Most states, though, provide home owners with legal protections designed to give them time to make good on their contract. Depending on state law, you have a certain amount of time—typically ninety days—to "cure" the mortgage by making up the delinquent payments. Accordingly, most lenders wait four or five months before accelerating the loan or starting **foreclosure**.

If you can't cure the mortgage within the specified time, the lender has a right to accelerate the mortgage, declaring the entire amount due. Unless you can come up with the money, the lender may then foreclose on the property and order it sold. Because many states require a judicial foreclosure in which all parties come before a judge, the process takes eight months to a year, although it may take less time if you're not living in the home.

If your property is sold at a public auction and the proceeds aren't enough to cover your principal and back interest, plus late charges, legal costs, and unpaid property taxes, the lender may still come after you for the difference, called a **deficiency**. You'd have no home but still owe a chunk of money.

If your lender is starting foreclosure, one way to salvage your credit record is to put the house on the market immediately. Sell it as fast as you can, even if you have to cut the price terribly. Then use the proceeds to pay off your mortgage (assuming you can sell the house for at least what you still owe). You can do this right up to the end of the redemption period. In many cases, lenders back off to allow time for the house to sell; after all, it's likely to net them more money than a sheriff's sale. And you may come out of it with enough to start over.

Another option if you don't have much equity in the home is just to hand your deed over to the lender and call it even. The lender might be willing to clean up your credit record in exchange for the deed, to save the time and trouble of foreclosure.

Fending off Foreclosure

If you expect trouble making payments, though, don't just let it slide and hope your lender doesn't notice.

Begin by negotiating with your lender. Explain the situation and see whether the lender is willing to adjust your payment schedule, lower your interest rate temporarily, or let you make payments only on the interest until you're back on your feet. Not all lenders are willing to do this, but many would rather help you work through this difficult time than go to the expense of foreclosure, then lose again when the home is sold by the sheriff for less than it's worth.

If your lender won't budge, see a mortgage broker or a different lending institution about taking out a loan based on the equity you have in your home. Use that loan to make your primary mortgage payments. The rates and fees for such loans are pretty high, but getting one may buy you some time.

During this period, watch out for con artists who get wind of your troubles and promise to help you with various quick remedies. Some claim they can arrange refinancing, while others say they can get you a loan to pay off your debts. Supposedly you'll be borrowing someone else's credit by obtaining a cosigner on a new loan, who will cure the default and make payments for several additional months until you're back on your feet and able to start repaying.

These deals, known as "equity skimming," actually involve selling the house for less than it's worth and leasing it back to you. You get to stay in the house as a tenant, under a lease that gives you an option to buy the house back within a certain number of months. Your rent covers the new mortgage payments. But like any tenant, you could be evicted if you can't fork over the rent.

The real catch is that option to buy it back. The deal expires in six, twelve, or eighteen months, at which time you have to come up with enough money to pay for the entire house—or it's gone. Of course, given the financial troubles that led you into this mess in the first place, there's no way you are likely to obtain that kind of money unless a rich uncle dies; no bank is going to lend you what you need. The result is that the kindly soul who offered to help you with your problems has actually cheated you out of your house. You don't even get your equity back.

These deals are patently illegal because they defraud the hapless home owner. Such a transaction has all the trappings of a loan—and that's what the home owner thinks it is, but it's really a sale and leaseback. The perpetrator's real purpose is to get your home for next to nothing.

Bankruptcy

If you're having trouble making mortgage payments, you may also be in trouble with credit cards, auto loans, back taxes, and other debt. Creditors are beating down your door and you don't know what to do.

Now's the time to discuss your options with an experienced bankruptcy lawyer. If you're poor or unemployed, you may be entitled to free legal services; consult your local legal aid office.

Although you'd never want to damage your credit rating unnecessarily, our country's bankruptcy laws can protect you from losing everything to your creditors. By taking some steps before it's too late, chances are you can save your home.

Bankruptcy can take several forms, depending on whether you're an individual or a business, how much debt is involved, and what you want to accomplish. For home owners, the basic options are Chapter 7 and Chapter 13.

- **Chapter 7 bankruptcy**, also called a straight bankruptcy, discharges most of your debts. Alimony, child support, student loans that have been due less than seven years, most taxes, and certain other debts can't be discharged. Any assets you have that aren't exempted by law are turned over to a bankruptcy trustee to divide up among your creditors.

  What you can keep depends on where you live. Although the Federal Bankruptcy Code keeps most aspects of bankruptcy uniform throughout the country, exemption laws vary wildly from state to state. If you go bankrupt in Delaware, you may keep only $500 in personal possessions, including schoolbooks, clothing, tools, a piano, a sewing machine, and the family Bible. In Virginia, you can keep, among other essentials, a cow and a calf, three hogs, and a horse.

  Some states have a **homestead exemption** that allows you either to keep your home or to retain a certain amount of equity in it, in addition to ordinary household furnishings, tools of your trade, and personal items. In Texas, Iowa, and Florida, for instance, you can keep your home no matter how much it's worth and how much equity you have in it, although you still have to pay any mortgages on it. Texas, which was settled by debtors, also allows the retention of an acre of land in the city or two hundred rural acres, plus $60,000 worth of personal property. In Illinois, you're allowed only $7,500 of equity per person or $15,000 per couple. In Georgia, the homestead exemption is only $5,000. In many states, the home owner must be the head of a family to get a homestead exemption.

  Your bankruptcy attorney will advise you on the steps you need to take to claim the homestead exemption. If this claim is not made correctly, one of your creditors may force the sale of your home.

  If the equity you have in your home is below the maximum allowed in your state's homestead exemption, you could declare bankruptcy with respect to your other debts but **reaffirm** your home mortgage, which means you must keep making payments on it in exchange for being able to retain the property. Most people who do this figure that going bankrupt on their other debts will make them better able to save their home.

If you have more equity than your state allows you to keep and the bankruptcy trustee in your area is aggressive, you may be required to sell your home to pay your creditors. But if you're in that position, a competent lawyer will advise you to stay away from Chapter 7. That's when Chapter 13 makes more sense.

- **Chapter 13 bankruptcy** is a way of reorganizing your debts to allow you to pay most of them and work your way through this difficult time. It's designed for individuals and mom-and-pop businesses with less than one million dollars in debt. Chapter 13 works only if you'll be earning money steadily during the term of the bankruptcy.

Basically, the law requires you to submit a plan for making payments on your debts over the next three or five years. During that period, as long as the plan has been approved by the bankruptcy trustee and you're abiding by it, creditors can't hound you, garnish your wages, or sue for payment. It's not up to your mortgage lender or other creditors to approve your plan or deny it. If it complies with the law, your creditors have no choice in the matter.

A typical reorganization plan, drawn up with the help of an attorney who specializes in bankruptcies, provides for paying secured creditors what they're owed, or at least the value of the collateral, and paying unsecured creditors a percentage of what they're owed.

Chapter 13 is a tool often used to help beleaguered home owners keep their homes. After all, if you lose your home because of bankruptcy, chances are you won't be able to buy another one for a very long time. Most lenders refuse to issue mortgages to people who've declared bankruptcy until a good two or three years after they're out of bankruptcy.

Here's how Chapter 13 works. Suppose you're three mortgage payments behind and your lender is talking foreclosure. Get a good lawyer and file for Chapter 13. The lawyer will help you figure out how much of your income you need for regular mortgage payments and living expenses and how much you could apply to your debts.

When you draw up the plan for repaying creditors, include those three payments along with your other debt. But inform your lender that you'll be keeping up with future payments, making one payment per month as usual outside the plan. That way you can make up the missed payments bit by bit over three to five years, along with back taxes, missing payments on your auto loan, and maybe some money toward credit card debt. You'll cure the default on your mortgage, so the lender will no longer be in a position to foreclose.

It's possible to file Chapter 13 after foreclosure, or even during your redemption period. Doing so puts the brakes on the whole process and buys you time to get your affairs back in order.

Of course, Chapter 13 is still a form of bankruptcy and it wreaks havoc with your credit rating. It'll take years to rebuild your credibility, even after you've worked through the plan. And Chapter 13 plans have a high failure rate; it takes a lot of hard work to make a go of them. Still, in many cases Chapter 13 is your best bet for saving your house and getting on with some semblance of a normal life.

PAYING OFF YOUR MORTGAGE

What if you're on the other side of the prosperity curve and have enough money to pay down your mortgage earlier than scheduled? Should you pay it off completely and be done with it? That depends on your circumstances. It's usually a good idea to make extra payments on your principal if you can, because that can reduce the term of the loan by several years and save you a bundle in interest. It's easiest to keep track of if you make each prepayment for the exact amount of principal due the following month. For each of these payments, you cut a month off the term of the loan.

Whether to pay off your loan completely depends on how much extra money you have. It's not a good idea to pay off your mortgage if it's going to leave you strapped for cash; you may need a cushion later for emergencies. If you're paying relatively high interest, you might want to refinance the loan to get a better rate (see above).

When you make that final payment, get a **Certificate of Satisfaction of Mortgage** (sometimes called a **Deed of Reconveyance** or a **Release of Deed**). This document states that the loan has been paid in full. Have it signed by the lender, notarized, and entered in the public records. If you've been paying to a previous owner rather than a bank, this document is just as important as one from a bank. Ask your lawyer to draw up the certificate, then send it with a return envelope. If the seller balks, ask your lawyer to apply a bit more pressure, because it's important for you to have that document.

If the bank agrees to file the document, wait a few months and then check with the county register of deeds to make sure it's been done. If not, do it yourself. If the lender was holding an abstract for your property, you should get it back now. If you were paying into an escrow account for tax and insurance bills, ask to see what's left in your account and get a refund.

Then sit back and relax. Legally you've been a home owner for years, but now your home really and truly is yours.

■

CHAPTER NINE

Death and Taxes

How Home Ownership Affects Your Tax Bill

"**B**UT IN THIS WORLD nothing can be said to be certain, except death and taxes," wrote Ben Franklin in 1789. But just as good health and medicine can help you postpone death, good advice and record keeping can help you reduce some taxes and postpone others.

That's especially true for you, the owner of that special place where you put your feet up. In the words of the late Sylvia Porter, personal finance guru, "Uncle Sam loves a home owner." It's our national policy that home ownership is good for the country, so (in a rare show of consistency) federal tax laws encourage people to buy and keep their own homes. This chapter will point out some of the tax breaks that may be available to you as a home owner. It's no great surprise, though, that what the government gives with one hand, it takes away with the other. Home owners may get breaks on their income taxes, but they have to ante up for state and local property taxes. Fortunately some localities provide property tax relief for particular types of home owners, such as farmers or owner-occupants, and almost all states equalize the tax burden by requiring local governments to maintain the same level of assessment for everyone. Still, assessors do make errors. The final section of this chapter will explain the assessment process and what steps you can take if your tax bill seems unreasonably high.

INCOME-TAX DEDUCTIONS

Let's begin, though, with federal income taxes. Numerous deductions are available for the home owner, some more significant than others. As you know, a deduction is an amount of money you subtract from your taxable income, thereby lowering the amount you have to pay. The federal government allows certain deductions in hopes of advancing particular social goals such as allowing people to provide for their children. In your case, the social goal is encouraging home ownership.

While the easiest way to do your taxes is just to claim the standard deduction, the only way to take advantage of the tax breaks described below is to itemize. That means more work and more careful recordkeeping, but it's time well spent because of the significance of the tax savings.

Here are some deductions that may be available to you. Remember that tax law is constantly changing, so don't rely on anything but the most recent IRS publications. They're available free from your local IRS office, or you can call 1-800-TAX-FORM (1-800-829-3676).

Property Taxes

The good news about having to pay state and local property taxes is that you can deduct them on your federal tax return. Keep track of what you pay (whether directly or through your mortgage lender's escrow account) and enter it in the appropriate place on your income tax form. Water and sewer charges, which generally are not measured by the value of the affected property, are not deductible.

Mortgage Interest

The biggest break for home owners is that you can deduct all the interest paid on a mortgage loan incurred to buy, build, or improve your home, up to $1 million. That's especially helpful in the first few years of your mortgage, when nearly every dollar of every mortgage payment you make goes to interest, not principal. Since many people put a quarter to a third of their incomes into mortgage payments, having such a big percentage be essentially tax-free is good news indeed.

This deduction applies to vacation homes, including condominiums and cooperative apartments, as long as they're not classified as business property (you must occupy the home at least fourteen days per year, or 10 percent of its rental time, to qualify for residential tax breaks). The same goes if your second home is a houseboat or motor home. If you own two homes, you can deduct up to $1 million in mortgage interest between them.

If you increase your mortgage when you refinance your home, interest on the increase is not deductible unless the increase qualifies as a home-equity loan or you use the extra proceeds for home improvements.

Loan Fees

If your mortgage deal required you to pay loan origination fees, better known as points, those fees are deductible on that year's tax return. This provision didn't apply to VA and FHA loans closed before December 3, 1990, though. Note also that you can only deduct closing costs for your principal residence, not your vacation home.

Points may likewise be deductible when you refinance, but the deduction must be spread over the entire term of the loan. If you later refinance again, though, you can probably deduct the remaining portion of the points from the prior refinance. The rules here are complicated, so talk to a tax professional or IRS representative about your particular circumstances.

Interest on Home-Equity Loans

If you take out a home-equity loan of up to $100,000, you can deduct the interest no matter what you do with the money. The total debt, though, may not exceed the fair market value of your home.

Rental Units

What if you rent out your basement apartment or the other half of your duplex? Rules for business property apply to that portion of your home, allowing you to deduct fire insurance premiums, utilities, repairs, depreciation, and similar expenses as well as mortgage interest and property taxes. Consult IRS Publication 527, *Residential Rental Property*, for details.

When you sell your home, though, you can't defer taxes on a capital gain from the portion of your property that isn't your residence (see below). Some tax professionals advise home owners to consider converting the rental or business portion of their home to residential use prior to sale, so they can defer taxes on the whole property.

Vacation Home Expenses

People often offset the cost of their resort condo or lakeside cabin by renting it out part of the year. Accordingly, tax law treats a vacation home as a hybrid of a residence and a business property. Which expenses are deductible depends on how many weeks per year the property is used by you or your relatives, and how many weeks it's rented out.

Suppose you rent it less than fifteen days per year. You don't have to report rental income, but you can only deduct mortgage interest, property taxes, and casualty losses (see below). At the other end of the spectrum, suppose you or your family don't use it more than fourteen days (or 10 percent of the days it was occupied). In that case, while you'd have to report rental income, essentially all the expenses of maintaining the property are deductible. The IRS recognizes a couple of categories in between with corresponding rules; consult IRS Publication 527 for details.

Leased Land

If you own a home that stands on leased ground, you may be able to deduct the rent you pay for the land. The Internal Revenue Code generally allows ground-rent deductions for leases of fifteen years or more that include an option to buy the land. When you buy the land, though, your payments aren't tax deductible.

Casualty Losses

If your home is damaged by a natural disaster such as fire, flood, or tornado, and the loss isn't fully covered by insurance, your out-of-pocket expenses may qualify as a deductible casualty loss. The same goes if a burglar breaks in and steals your uninsured diamond ring. Note that casualty losses are one-time occurrences; sustained damage, say by termites or slowly leaking pipes, doesn't count.

You have to take the deduction in the year the loss occurred unless your home is in a national disaster area, where records may have been lost. In that case, you can amend the previous year's return to claim the deduction.

Any insurance reimbursements or federal disaster relief grants are subtracted from the casualty loss, along with a $100 deductible. Then you multiply your household's adjusted gross income by 10 percent; only casualty losses exceeding that figure can be deducted.

You may not be able to deduct much casualty loss if your home wasn't worth much to begin with. Deductible losses are limited to the difference between the home's market value right before the damage and its market value right after, as determined by an appraiser. If the home's adjusted basis (its original cost plus improvements) is even less than the market-value calculation, the adjusted basis serves as the limit for deductible casualty losses. For more on a home's basis, see the next section.

Likewise, note that casualty losses are among the itemized deductions that are only deductible to the extent that they exceed 2 percent of your income.

Home Office

If you run a business from your home, your office expenses are probably deductible. Depending on the size of your home and how much of it is designated office space, the deduction can be significant enough to justify the extra effort needed to qualify. If your office meets the standards spelled out by the IRS, you can deduct the cost of repairs, furniture, computers and office equipment, extra telephone lines, and other business-related expenses. You can also deduct a proportional share of your home's **depreciation** (ordinary wear and tear), utility bills, and insurance. Be aware, though, that you can deduct no more than your business actually generated.

Although you can no longer deduct the entire cost of a desk or computer the first year, you may claim **accelerated depreciation** if you use the item more than 50 percent of the time for your business. This allows you to claim most of the deduction the first two years.

The IRS, however, reserves the right to declare that your "business" is really a hobby, or that your home office doesn't meet its rather stringent standards for deductible business use of the home. (For more on IRS standards in this area, see box, opposite.)

Historic Homes

If your home is listed in the *National Register of Historic Places* or stands in a historic district, you may be able to deduct some of the costs of rehabilitating your home—but only if you rent part of it out. Otherwise, the IRS considers your rehab costs to be personal expenses, not business expenses.

If you grant a façade easement to a historic preservation association, restricting yourself and all future owners from changing your home's façade, you may be able to deduct any loss in the home's market value as a charitable deduction. Figuring out how your home might be more valuable if its façade were changed is a bit speculative, though; better get professional help.

WHEN YOU SELL

Most year-to-year deductions are small potatoes compared to the biggest tax liability home owners face: tax on their capital gain when they sell the house. Any time you sell property for more than you paid for it, whether it's a stock portfolio or the family bungalow, Uncle Sam wants a slice of the pie. Since a house purchased for $40,000 in the 1950s might be worth $200,000 or more today, the income tax on that much gain could be staggering. Fortunately, the federal government provides some protection for those pursuing the American dream of moving up, and for golden agers who want to sell the family home and live off the proceeds.

YOUR HOME OFFICE

So you've started a home-based business, selling wallpaper supplies or writing brochures for local merchants. You turn the spare bedroom into an office. Can you deduct office costs as a business expense?

Yes, if you meet the following tests:

- *Your business has to generate a profit at least two out of five years. Otherwise, the IRS may consider it a hobby, not a business.*

- *Your home has to be (a) the principal place of business for the operation, (b) the place you meet patients, clients, or customers if you deal with them in person, or (c) in a separate structure not attached to your home. This can be sticky for professionals who spend most of their time meeting patients or clients elsewhere but do their book work in one of the rooms at home. Even if they have no other office to do it in, the IRS doesn't allow deductions for home office expenses, on the grounds that your home office is not your principal place of business.*

- *The space must be used regularly as an office. Part-time work is fine, as long as it's regular.*

- *The office must be used exclusively for the business. The IRS frowns on claims that the den is a law office if it's also the family TV room. One exception is home day care, which often takes place in rooms the family uses during off hours. In that case, you figure what percentage of the time it's used for day care purposes and deduct that percentage of the expenses for those rooms.*

- *If you work as an employee, your working at home must be for the convenience of your employer.*

For more information, consult IRS Publication 587, Business Use of Your Home.

"Basis" and Other Basics

First, though, be sure you understand how the government computes capital gain. The key concept is your home's **basis**. This is the price you paid for the house back when you bought it, or, if you inherited it, what it was appraised for at that time. If you

TAXING THE HOUSEKEEPER

In the early days of the Clinton Administration, a nominee to the office of attorney general was forced to withdraw because she had failed to pay employment taxes for her child's nanny. Whether or not you're a candidate for public office, you can get in trouble with the IRS for failing to pay Social Security and Medicare taxes for people who work in your house, whether you hire a full staff of gardeners, butlers, and maids or just a housekeeper who comes in for a few hours a week.

The regulations are stricter than you might expect. The IRS considers you an employer if a worker performs services that are subject to your will and control as to what must be done and how to do it. A lawn-care service that provides its own tools and laborers would not be the homeowner's employee, but a once-a-week housekeeper subject to the homeowner's supervision would be.

However, in 1994 Congress changed the law to ease the filing requirements for those who employ domestic workers. In 1994, you were required to pay Social Security taxes to the IRS for every employee who made more than $1,000 a year (the amount will be adjusted annually for inflation). However, no taxes are owed for domestic employees under the age of eighteen whose primary occupation is not domestic work.

Failing to pay these taxes could lead to fines. The IRS can't necessarily tell who hires a housekeeper and who doesn't, but certain inconsistencies serve as red flags. For instance, if you claim a deduction for in-home child care but neglect to pay employment taxes on your nanny, you might be in hot water. Ditto if you include the cost of a housekeeper in your home office deductions but fail to withhold.

IRS Publication 926, Employment Taxes for Household Employees, *tells how much to withhold and what to send where.*

built your home, it's the cost of the land at the time plus all costs of construction. The basis is increased by certain types of home improvements. Likewise, the basis is decreased by uninsured casualty losses, such as the garage being washed away by a flood.

The higher your basis, the smaller your gain, which is the difference between your basis and what you sell the house for. The smaller the gain, the less tax you have to pay. So it's a good idea to keep track of improvements that might increase your home's basis. These are alterations that either increase its value, extend its life, or alter its uses, such as adding a bathroom, landscaping the yard, building in bookcases, wallpapering the bedrooms or even putting brass numbers by the front door. Pay for such work by check, get a receipt, and keep it in a file where you can use it later to prove that your home's basis has increased. Note that mere repairs, such as fixing leaky pipes or reshingling the roof, don't count. But if you package a bunch of repairs and call it an "extensive remodeling or restoration," the IRS is willing to adjust your basis upward.

While a routine paint or plaster repair job wouldn't normally affect your basis, fix-up costs that you incur within ninety days of signing a contract for sale can be figured in when you're calculating the profit on the sale. So can real estate commissions, attorney's fees, title insurance, local transfer taxes, and other costs of selling. So while long-term home improvements serve to increase the home's basis, fix-up costs reduce your profit on the sale and accordingly reduce your tax liability.

Your adjusted basis gets carried over to subsequent homes as you defer tax on capital gain (see below). In case of an audit, the IRS expects you to keep track of each house you buy and sell: what you paid for it, what improvements you added, and what you sold it for. Good recordkeeping is really important.

Deferring Capital Gain

Now, about those protections. First, you can defer payment of tax on capital gain if you buy or build another main home within two years before or after selling the old one (longer for military personnel). Deferring payment of taxes as long as possible is almost always a good deal, because eventually you'll be in a lower tax bracket. Besides, the same dollar amount probably won't be worth as much thirty years from now.

The key provision is that you can only defer the cost of the new house. That's no problem if it cost more than you sold the old one for, but if it cost less, you can defer only a portion of the capital gains. Say you originally bought your home for $100,000 and sold it for $200,000—you have a gain of $100,000. If your new home costs at least $200,000, you can defer the whole gain. But if it costs $175,000, you can defer only $75,000 of the gain.

Note that this door doesn't swing both ways. If you lose money on the sale of your home, you can't deduct the loss and pay less in taxes.

Win or lose, whenever you sell a home you have to file Form 2199, reporting the sale date, the price, and how much profit is subject to immediate taxation, if any. This one-page form takes you through the calculations required to determine gain on sale, adjusted sales price, taxable gain, and the adjusted basis of your new home. If your new home costs less than the adjusted sales price of your old home, you might have to pay some tax now while deferring the rest. If you die without selling the home, all

- *If the IRS wants to question you about your tax records, it must set a reasonable time and place. You can bring your attorney or accountant, and tape record the entire proceeding (at your expense).*

- *In the past, some field offices have evaluated their agents' performance based on how much tax money they collect. Quota systems are now illegal, and field officials must file periodic statements that they do not use quotas.*

- *You now have a right to sue the IRS for damages if one of its agents, in the process of collecting taxes, recklessly or intentionally disregards the tax code.*

- *If you've entered an agreement with the IRS to pay your taxes over time, the agency cannot cancel the agreement without notice even if your finances have improved. They can cancel the agreement if you fail to make payments, but they must follow procedures set out in the new law.*

- *Before seizing your bank account or other property to pay back taxes, the IRS must provide thirty days notice rather than ten. The amount of wages and property exempt from levies, such as tools and equipment needed for the taxpayer's trade or business, has also been increased.*

capital gains taxes are wiped off the slate. Your beneficiaries will inherit it at a new, stepped-up basis, and they don't have to pay any tax on capital gains accumulated on the sale of your home or homes over the years.

What if you own a duplex, live in one unit and rent out the other? In that case, you can only defer capital gain on the half you use as your residence. The other is a business property, not subject to this tax break.

The $125,000 Exclusion

Now for the other big protection. Taxation on capital gain can represent a disaster for older people whose home has increased dramatically in value over the years as real estate prices have escalated. When it's finally time to sell the place and move into an apartment or retirement community, these people may face a monstrous tax on capital gain that they're especially ill-equipped to pay.

To avoid that scenario, the federal government allows Americans fifty-five and over to exclude up to $125,000 in gain when they sell their home—but they can only do so one time. Form 2119, which every homeowner has to file to report the sale of a home, includes a section giving those fifty-five and over the option of excluding that much of their gain. (If there's more than $125,000 in gain, they pay tax on the difference unless they roll it over into a new residence.)

One time means one time. Married couples get only one exclusion between them, which they can take when either spouse reaches fifty-five. If they divorce, each gets to exclude $125,000 in gain—provided the home isn't sold until after the divorce is final. If, say, the ex-husband uses his exclusion then later remarries, his new wife is precluded from claiming an exclusion. Accordingly, if you're planning to sell your home and marry someone who's already used his exclusion, either sell the home before you get married or make sure you keep the title in your name only.

The $125,000 exclusion applies only to your principal residence, and only if you've actually been living in it three of the five years before you sold it. If you decide to rent it out for five or six years and then sell it, you can't then take your $125,000 exclusion on the gain.

Plan ahead to get the maximum benefit from this exclusion. A good strategy is to keep deferring taxes on your profits (by purchasing more expensive homes) until you make your final move, say from the executive estate to a small condo. By that time you'll have accumulated a series of profits; take the exclusion then.

For details on IRS regulations in this area, see Publication 523, *Selling Your Home*.

PROPERTY TAXES

Our country had property taxes before it was a country; the Massachusetts Bay Colony levied a tax to pay government expenses back in 1692. In every state in the union, property taxes provide much of the revenue used for schools, police protection,

TAXING THE CONDO

If you live in a condominium or cooperative, here are some special tax considerations.

- *The homeowners' association must file a tax return to report any income, such as interest income on the association's bank account. If the association has very little income, files annually as a tax-exempt organization, and if 90 percent of its expenses are for common element maintenance, the simple Form 1120 is enough. Otherwise, the association must file corporate Form 1120.*

- *If your condominium's common elements are upgraded, say with new windows throughout, your share of the expense can be added to your unit's cost basis for tax purposes. Such improvements add to the value of your unit, so they increase the basis (original cost plus improvements). That's good, because then you'll effectively have less profit when you sell the place, so will owe less tax on capital gain. Save your association's annual report, which should list common element improvements and their cost per unit.*

- *Property taxes on condominium or cooperative units reflect the size of each unit and each unit owner's share of the common elements. As with a house, check your statement to make sure you've been assessed correctly.*

firefighting, and other services. In forty-seven states, responsibility for assessment and administration of property taxes is shared between state and local governments. (In Maryland it's all done at the state level, while Delaware and Hawaii rely entirely on local efforts.)

While citizens disagree strongly on how much taxation is necessary for needed services, most would agree that the system should be fair, requiring owners of similar properties to pay similar tax levies. The collection of property taxes involves a complex process of assessment, though, and mistakes can be made. It's important to understand how the system works and what you can do if your tax bill seems to be out of line.

The Assessment Process

In most states it's up to the assessor or board of assessors, who are local government officials, to place a value on your property for tax purposes. Generally they follow a locally accepted formula for assigning value. The local government then imposes a certain amount of tax per dollar of assessed value, which results in the tax bill you receive in the mail.

The process of arriving at individual property tax bills is rather complex. Each property in a municipality is described on a "property record card," which includes a legal description of the land and a description of the buildings and other improvements on the land, which probably indicates square footage, construction materials, depreciation, and other physical attributes. The card may include a recent sale price or the assessor's estimate of the value of the improvements based on replacement cost. If the owner has taken out a building permit for a big addition, that might be noted on the card too. Each property is reassessed on a regular basis, whether every year or every four years.

In big metropolitan areas, there are simply too many homes to assess each one based on its individual characteristics. Instead, the assessor might use a mass appraisal method, assigning a value per square foot for a given neighborhood.

There's usually a complicated schedule for getting from appraised value to the dollar amount of taxes owed. In many states the actual value is reduced by a certain percentage, then multiplied by the local millage rate. (Millage is a common method for determining property tax. A mill is one one-thousandth of a dollar. So if your town taxes eight mills and your property is valued for tax purposes at $100,000, you'd owe $800.) After crunching all the numbers, city employees send you a notice of assessed value, followed before long by the actual tax bill. If it looks reasonable to you, you pay the bill and that's the end of it.

Fighting City Hall

But what if you think the tax levy is out of line? What if the assessment has jumped dramatically since last year? Or what if property values in your neighborhood have plummeted but the assessment hasn't?

The time of object is when you receive notice of assessed value. Most likely you have a given time period to object and try to convince the assessors to change their minds. If you wait to receive the actual tax bill, it may be too late.

At this stage, procedures are informal. You may want a lawyer to help you set up the best case, but many home owners represent themselves. Your job is to gather any evidence you think will show that your property isn't worth as much as the assessor thinks it is, and to present your argument in a clear, rational manner.

Here's what you might want to look at:

- **Assessment notice.** Look for obvious mistakes in the notice you received, such as an incorrect address or the wrong number of bedrooms.

- **Property record card.** Go down to the assessor's office and ask to see your property record card. Make sure the acreage, square footage, and other details are correct.

- **Special tax breaks.** Some jurisdictions give tax breaks to certain categories of property owners such as a 10 percent tax waiver for owner-occupied homes or for disabled veterans. Ask the assessor's office what breaks you qualify for and make sure that exemption is reflected in the assessment notice. Tax breaks aren't given automatically; you must apply for them.

- **Purchase contracts** and closing statements showing that the house changed hands recently at a lower price than the assessed value.

- **Property condition.** Is your home overrun by termites or badly damaged by fire? The assessor might not know about it. Take repair estimates or photos with you to show that your house isn't worth what the assessor claims it is.

- **Comparable homes.** Do a bit of research to learn what similar homes in your neighborhood have sold for recently. Local real estate brokers should have sales information, or check with the county registrar of deeds. You can even ask at the assessor's office to see the assessed value of comparable homes. Be sure you have the address of each house you talk about, and if possible the permanent index number (available from the county collector's office or the township assessor).

- **Appraisal.** If the amount in dispute is significant enough and you're pretty sure you're right, you may want to hire an appraiser to provide a second opinion on the value of the property. When choosing an appraiser, look for someone well qualified, with a reputation for competence, who would be credible as a witness if the matter winds up in court.

If your negotiations with the assessor don't go your way, you may be able to appeal the decision through an equalization board, assessment review board, or board of appeals. Some jurisdictions have a taxpayer's advocate to take your side and help you through the process. Again, you'd present your evidence and explain why you believe your assessment should be lowered.

If that doesn't work but you really want to push it further, the next step is to take your evidence to a state court or tax tribunal. Consult your lawyer or local government officials to find out what your options are and how to proceed.

If you engage a lawyer to argue your case before the assessor or the review board, you'll probably have to pay a percentage of your tax savings in legal fees. If you win, though, you may well save several hundred dollars per year.

CHAPTER TEN

■

Getting Older

Special Concerns of Aging Home Owners

"LIFE BEGINS WHEN the kids move out and the dog dies." For many Americans, there's a fair bit of truth to that slogan. Some 80 percent of the retirees surveyed recently for the American Association of Retired Persons owned their own homes, three quarters of them free and clear. For many, a lifetime of earning and investing has provided a tidy income to spend on travel and recreation. Their biggest choices for the near future may be whether to stay in their well-tended Colonial near the kids or move to a beachfront condo in some tropical paradise.

For others, the "golden years" have turned to brass. The death of a husband or wife has made the family home a lonely place to be. Inflation has eroded their savings, leaving them property-rich but cash-poor. Joints ache, eyes go bad, and plans for celebrating retirement turn into worries about long-term care.

Now's the time to consider ways to increase your income without having to sell your house. Home-equity conversion plans from reverse mortgages to charitable annuities can offer the best of both worlds: a steady income to cover all those expenses, and a chance to keep on living in the home you love.

If the family home isn't meeting your needs anymore, it may be time to think about a move. Since your home has probably increased in value in recent years, selling it now could give you a nice chunk of money to invest in a more amenable place to live. Older Americans now have a wide range of options for housing, from retirement communities on the golf course to assisted-living apartments to continuing-care facilities and nursing homes.

This chapter explains some of the personal and financial decisions you'll need to make, the risks and benefits involved with various options, and your legal rights.

HOME-EQUITY CONVERSION

Suppose that after years of paying on the mortgage, you finally own your home outright. That's a nice, secure feeling, but it doesn't mean you have enough money to live on. Your assets are tied up in the house; they can't pay your electric bill or finance your trips to the supermarket. You don't want to sell the house, but it's hard to make ends meet. Take a look at **home-equity conversion plans**, which can help you add to your monthly income without having to leave your home.

These plans fall into two broad categories: loans and sales. Loan plans permit you to borrow against the equity in your home. They include reverse mortgages and special-purpose loans on which repayment is deferred. They should not be confused with "home-equity loans" and "home-equity lines of credit," which require you to make monthly payments or risk losing your house. Sale plans include **sale-leasebacks**, **life estates**, and **charitable annuities**. Let's consider each of these options.

Reverse Mortgages

A **reverse mortgage** lets you borrow against the equity in your home. It's a "rising-debt loan," which means that the interest is added to the principal loan balance each month because it isn't being paid. The interest keeps compounding, so the longer you have a reverse mortgage, the more you owe. But unless you agree to a specific loan term, the debt doesn't come due until you sell your home, move permanently, or die. In some new plans, you can continue to receive payments even if you move.

When the loan does come due, the amount to be repaid cannot exceed the appraised value of the property—because you use the proceeds of the sale to pay off the loan. Of course, that means you won't receive as much money from the sale; you'll already have spent it on living expenses.

QUESTIONS ABOUT REVERSE MORTGAGES

If I get a reverse mortgage on my home that pays regular income, will it affect my eligibility for Social Security or Medicare?

No, because these benefits are not based on need. The same goes for pensions you or your spouse have earned.

However, without careful planning, the income from a reverse mortgage could affect eligibility for Supplemental Security Income (SSI), Medicaid, food stamps, and some state benefit programs.

In general, reverse mortgage payments are considered to be a loan, and will not affect benefits if the money is spent during the month in which it is received. But if the money is not spent during that month, it will be counted as a resource, and may lead to termination of benefits. Be aware that payments received under the new reverse-annuity mortgage plans will be considered income, even if they are spent in the month in which they are received.

What are the tax consequences of a reverse mortgage?

There are two issues here. The first is whether the income from a reverse mortgage is taxed. So far it has not been, under the assumption that it's a loan advance. Second is whether the interest can be deducted. Generally, interest cannot be deducted until it is paid. Since the interest on a reverse mortgage is not paid until the loan comes due, it cannot be deducted until that time.

What happens when I die?

A reverse mortgage is really a loan that becomes due when you sell your home or die. The lender doesn't take title to your home, but your heirs have to pay it off. If they want to keep the family home, they could do that by refinancing the debt with a regular (forward) mortgage, provided they're eligible. Otherwise, they could sell it and use the proceeds to pay off the loan.

Depending on your needs and the deal you arrange, you can get a lump sum, receive monthly installments, or draw on a line of credit. The amount of the loan you will receive is based on your age, the value of your home and your equity, the interest rate, the term of the loan, and some other factors. Except for some special-purpose state plans, like those designed to pay for home repairs, there are no restrictions on how you use the money.

To get a reverse mortgage, you have to be at least sixty-two years old and own the property free and clear (except for liens or mortgages that can be paid off with proceeds from the loan). Unlike traditional loans or home-equity lines of credit, the lender doesn't care about your income. Only single-family residences (including some condominiums) are eligible; mobile homes, multifamily dwellings (including duplexes), and cooperatives are not. As with any loan, you have to pay origination fees and closing costs.

Reverse mortgages can be obtained in more than thirty-five states and the District of Columbia. Some states sponsor home repair plans that are essentially reverse mortgages. The most common product, though, is the federally insured Home-Equity Conversion Mortgage, or HECM. The federal government guarantees that you'll keep receiving your payments even if the lender defaults on your payments.

Then there are lender-insured plans. These include a mortgage-insurance premium and higher costs, so your loan balance grows faster. But you can usually get larger loan advances, and you may be able to mortgage less than the full value of your home.

Finally, there are uninsured plans. These are fixed-term loans, so you'd have to repay the whole amount (with interest) after a certain number of years. If you couldn't repay it, you'd have to sell your house and move.

A consumer guide entitled *Home Made Money* and a list of reverse-mortgage lenders is available from the American Association of Retired Persons, Consumer Affairs, 601 E. Street, N.W., Washington, D.C. 20049.

Sale-Leasebacks

In a **sale-leaseback**, you sell the equity in your home, but retain the right to continue living there, often paying a monthly rent. This approach is often used by the homeowner's grown son or daughter as a way of keeping the home in the family while providing retirement income for the parents.

The buyer (often your grown child) usually makes a substantial down payment to you, the home owner. You act as a lender by granting the buyer a mortgage. You receive the buyer's mortgage payments; the buyer receives your rent payments. You remain in the home and can use the down payment and the mortgage payments as income. The buyer can deduct the mortgage interest payment from his or her income, and will also benefit if the value of the property increases. Although family members are usually motivated by a desire to help, be aware that the IRS requires that both the sale price and the rental payments be fair-market rate. Before 1986, the tax laws made sale-leasebacks good investments, but there are fewer tax advantages now.

Life Estates

In a **life estate** (also called a **sale of a remainder interest**), you sell your home to a buyer but keep the right to live there during your lifetime. Again, this is most often arranged between parents and their grown children as part of their estate plan. Chances are you wouldn't find an outside investor to do this.

The buyer pays you a lump sum, monthly payments, or both. You are usually responsible for taxes and repairs while you live in the house. At your death, full ownership passes automatically to the buyer.

Charitable Remainder Trusts

Another possibility is a **charitable remainder trust**, in which you donate your home to a charity in return for a lifetime annuity and possibly a tax deduction. You keep a life estate, which means you can stay there as long as you live. You remain responsible for taxes and maintenance. When you die, your home becomes the property of the organization.

The down side is that your beneficiaries wouldn't inherit your home. If they have adequate resources of their own, though, this arrangement can be an excellent way to accomplish two goals: provide needed retirement income for yourself and give a significant gift to your favorite charity.

Home-Equity Loans

A traditional **home-equity loan** is very different from a reverse mortgage, and can be a risk for an older person on a fixed income. As with a reverse mortgage, you borrow against the equity you have built up in your home. But in a home-equity loan, you must make regular monthly payments or you may lose your home.

If you expect enough income to make the payments, though, these loans do have tax advantages. Since it's no longer possible to deduct interest on loans for consumer goods such as car loans and credit card bills, many home owners have turned to home-equity loans. With such loans, you can borrow up to $100,000 on the equity in your first and second homes, use the money for any purpose, and deduct all the interest you pay. You can even deduct the interest on a home-equity loan that exceeds $100,000 if you use the money for home improvements.

If you're not going to use such a large loan for home improvements and still want to deduct the interest, you must be able to prove that your home equity, plus improvements, equals the amount of the loan.

Government Benefits

Remember that home-equity conversion isn't the only way to increase your income. If you find that your monthly income doesn't meet your expenses, you may be eligible for government benefits such as Supplemental Security Income, food stamps, or Medicaid.

Some states also have property tax credit or deferral programs you may be eligible for. To find out more about these programs, call your local agency on aging.

Thinking about tapping your home's equity? Consider all of the available options before you make your decision. If you're already receiving public benefits, find out whether any home-equity conversion plan you choose has an effect on those benefits.

HOUSING OPTIONS

As you get older and your circumstances change, staying in the home you now own may no longer be ideal. Maybe you and your spouse are rattling around in the house you built years ago to rear your six children. Maybe your spouse has died and it's just too hard to stay in that house with all those memories. Maybe you'd rather be in a warmer climate with lots of like-minded people and a host of recreational facilities. Or maybe your health isn't what it used to be and you're afraid you'll soon need to be taken care of.

You have a wide range of choices, depending on your current and future health needs, your financial circumstances, and your personal preferences. One is to take advantage of new models for senior living in a home setting, with assistance as needed. These include:

- **Home-sharing programs** that match home owners with companionable people who are willing to pay rent or perform some services in exchange for housing.

- **Assisted living**, which combines a homelike setting with services designed to meet individual needs. These programs may be privately owned and operated, government-supported, or sponsored by religious or other nonprofit organizations. For information, contact your local agency on aging.

- **Elder Cottage Housing Opportunities** (ECHO units). These are small, attractive, manufactured homes that you can lease and install behind or beside a family member's house. When they're no longer needed, they can be removed and returned. They give you the opportunity to live independently, close to your loved ones but not right on top of them.

  Be aware that many communities have zoning ordinances that can be a barrier to even the most appealing little ECHO unit, because they're often classified as mobile homes and banned from single-family lots. The law in this area is still developing, so you may have to fight city hall for the right to live next to your family through this sensible solution. For more information, see the AARP publication, *Key Issues in Elder Cottage Housing Opportunity: Restrictions on Manufactured Housing.*

Moving to Paradise

A lot of adults dream of the day they can retire and move to that lakeside property they bought years ago. Others have always hated those cold midwestern winters and plan to buy a condo in Arizona. Although 86 percent of those interviewed for the AARP survey preferred to stay in their present home and never move, the dream of retiring somewhere better is alive and well. In fact, you can bet that some of those surveyed have already done just that!

If you're thinking of pulling up stakes and buying a new home somewhere else, chances are you've already checked out the climate and the scenery. Be sure, though, that you've considered all the other factors that can make or break your move. These include:

- **Cost of living.** Can you afford to live there? How do housing costs stack up against those in the area you're leaving? What do goods and services cost there? Before making your final decision, try subscribing to the local newspaper in your dream community to get a feel for the economic climate as well as the leisure opportunities.

- **State and local taxes.** Is there a state income tax, and do retirees get any special tax breaks? Is there a sales tax or a tax on stocks, bonds, and other "intangibles"? How about state inheritance tax? What can you expect in the way of property taxes? Is there an over–sixty-five exemption?

- **State tax policies.** If you move, will your former state keep taxing your retirement plan payouts? Some states do, figuring that you earned the money in their state so it's only fair. Some only tax lump-sum distributions. But as state budgets get tighter, more legislatures are likely to reach their hands into retirees' pension plans. If your old state taxes your pension plan, will your new state allow a credit?

- **Your kind of town?** Vacation in the areas you're considering at different times of the year, and talk to local residents about what they like and don't like. Then try renting for a few months; it's cheaper than buying a home and then deciding you don't like the area.

Retirement Communities

An increasingly popular alternative is moving into a community specifically designed to meet the needs of seniors. Among them is a wide range of architectural options, from high-rise developments to garden apartments on a wooded campus.

The modern model of a retirement community first sprang up in the 1950s in the Sun Belt states. Senior communities offered independent living beside the golf course, with a handy swimming pool and a full schedule of social activities. As the idea caught on all sorts of hybrids developed, offering choices that cover the gamut from independent living through total nursing care.

Facility definitions differ among states and sometimes even within states. For the sake of simplicity, let's consider three types of community along a continuum of services.

- **Independent living communities** offer little or no health and supportive services, although they may have recreational and social programs.

- **Continuing-care retirement communities (CCRCs)** provide a fairly extensive range of housing options, care and services, including nursing home services. You may be able to start out in a nice little apartment with a dining hall nearby, move to an assisted-living complex if you need it, and know you'll have a space in the community's nursing home if your health deteriorates.

- **Assisted-living communities** fall between these extremes. They offer a wide variety of housing and health or supportive services, but not nursing home care. Such facilities are also called "congregate care," "board and care," "personal care," and "housing with supportive services," among other names.

Most retirement communities are developed privately, although many are sponsored by nonprofit groups and agencies, including churches and charitable organizations. All states regulate one or more types of assisted living, and most states regulate continuing-care communities, but the extent of regulation varies considerably among states. Many independent-living communities are structured as conventional home ownership, legally no different from a standard real estate purchase and governed by local real estate law. Others have you rent your unit like any apartment, so the transaction is governed by landlord–tenant law. If you opt for either of these forms, you pay the cost of your mortgage or lease, plus condominium or association fees if applicable.

In facilities that promise additional services, facilities, or health care, the payment arrangement includes some mechanism to pay for these added benefits. There are four basic types of contract, distinguished by payment arrangement. Keep in mind, though, that state regulations may categorize facilities differently.

- **"Turnover of assets"** or **"total fee in advance"** contracts without monthly fees. These contracts are all but extinct today. They were common in the original continuing-care communities, often called "life care" communities, developed by religious or fraternal organizations. Residents turned all their assets over to the community in exchange for a lifetime of care. Many communities using this model failed, because the assets received by the sponsors were not sufficient to keep up with rising health care expenses of residents over their lifetimes.

- **Entrance fee plus monthly fee contracts.** Most continuing-care retirement facilities today charge an entrance fee ranging from $15,000 to over $200,000, essentially a partial prepayment for future services such as eye exams or personal care. This payment normally does not buy an interest in the real estate. Residency rights and obligations are governed by a long-term lease or occupancy agreement. Monthly fees are subject to periodic adjustments for inflation and, in some cases, for the resident's needed level of care. Increasingly CCRCs are providing greater refundability of entrance fees, even 100% refundability, but this usually results in higher monthly fees.

- **"Pay-as-you-go"** contracts. With no entrance fee, these contracts are essentially straight rental arrangements with a defined set of services available when needed for an additional charge. Most assisted-living and an increasing number of continuing-care facilities offer this arrangement. This type of contract involves the least initial investment, but is subject to greater changes in monthly fees, since the resident assumes all or most of the financial risk for services.

- **Condominiums or cooperatives with continuing-care contracts.** Retirement communities that offer an ownership interest to residents under a condominium or cooperative arrangement with a service package included are relatively new to the scene. These ownership/contractual arrangements are unavoidably complex and bring with them special advantages and risks.

Another way to categorize continuing-care retirement communities is by how much nursing care is prepaid. The American Association of Homes for the Aging distinguishes three types:

- **Type A communities**, the most expensive, guarantee as much care as the resident might need, for as long as needed. They provide two or three meals per day, and may require residents to buy a certain number of meals per month.

- **Type B communities** sell contracts guaranteeing a specified number of days of nursing care, either per year or throughout the resident's lifetime. After that, the resident (or her family) must pay for daily fees. Personal services may not be covered by the monthly fees.

- **Type C communities** offer nursing care on a pay-per-day basis. Likewise, meals and personal care are rarely included in the basic monthly fees.

All these potential differences could add up to a confusing number of choices. Not that you'd seriously consider every possible community; most people are limited by their chosen city or state and look at just a few. But be sure you know what the fee and service arrangements are for any community you're considering.

After all, moving into a continuing-care community is a major financial investment, which may well use up all or most of your financial resources. You may not be able to get your money back. Consider it carefully, visit the facility at length, talk to both staff and residents, and seek professional advice from a lawyer or financial advisor before you make a commitment.

Here are some questions to ask:

- What is the provider's background and experience? The provider is the person or entity legally and financially responsible for providing continuing care. Some facilities advertise that they are "sponsored" by nonprofit groups or churches that in reality have no legal control or financial responsibility. Be wary if such illusory sponsorship is trumpeted in sales literature.

- Is the provider financially sound? Have the facility's financial, actuarial, and operating statements been reviewed by a professional? Determine whether it has sufficient financial reserves.

- Are all levels of care licensed or certified under applicable state statutes?

- How does the facility ensure the quality of care and services provided? Is it accredited by any recognized private accrediting organization?

- What is the entrance fee, and when can you get all or part of it back? The facility should provide a formula for a *pro rata* refund of the entrance fee based on the resident's length of stay, regardless of whether the facility or the resident initiates the termination. Some facilities offer the option of fully refundable entrance fees.

- What is the monthly fee? When and how much can it be increased? What happens if fee increases exceed your ability to pay? Some facilities have a program that grants financial assistance to residents whose income becomes inadequate to pay increasing monthly fees and personal expenses.

- Will fees change when your living arrangements or level-of-care needs change? That is, what happens to the fee if you have to transfer from independent living to assisted living or nursing care?

- What does your living unit consist of, and to what extent can you change or redecorate it?

- What happens if you marry, divorce, become widowed, or wish to have a friend or family member move in?

- Exactly what services are included in your regular fees? What costs extra, and how much? What limitations apply? (See box, opposite, for a checklist of things to look for.)

- Does the facility provide a nursing unit? What happens if a bed is not available when you need it?

A CHECKLIST FOR RETIREMENT COMMUNITY SERVICES

If you're thinking of moving into a continuing-care community or nursing home, inquire about coverage, limitations, and costs of the following matters:

- *Meal services*
- *Special diets/tray service*
- *Utilities*
- *Cable television*
- *Furnishings*
- *Unit maintenance*
- *Linens/personal laundry*
- *Housekeeping*
- *Recreational/cultural activities*
- *Transportation*
- *Physician services*
- *Nursing care facility services*
- *Nursing services outside a nursing unit (e.g., assistance with medications)*
- *Private duty nursing*
- *Dental and eye care*
- *Personal care services (i.e., assistance with eating, dressing, bathing, toileting, etc.)*
- *Homemaker/companion services*
- *Drugs, medication, and medical equipment/supplies*

- To what extent does the facility have the right to change the fees? Can it cut back, change or eliminate services?
- Does the facility limit its responsibility for certain health conditions or preexisting conditions? When can you become too sick or impaired to be cared for by the facility? A preexisting health condition is one diagnosed or treated in a certain period of time before entering the facility.

FINDING A RETIREMENT FACILITY

- *The American Association of Homes for the Aging publishes* The Consumer's Directory of Continuing Care Retirement Communities, *profiling not-for-profit retirement communities around the country and providing an overview of CCRC types, terminology, and features that consumers might want to consider. For ordering information, contact AAHA Publications, 901 E Street, N.W., Suite 500, Washington, D.C. 20004; 202-783-2242.*

- *The American Association of Retired Persons maintains a computer data base of retirement housing, including CCRCs and assisted living, and will provide a free printout for your geographic area. Request a printout (and specify your geographic area) from Membership Communications, AARP, 601 E Street, N.W., Washington, D.C. 20049; 202-434-2277.*

- *State or local agencies on aging frequently prepare directories or guides on housing options for older persons and persons with disabilities. Find the agency's number in your local phone book.*

- Can you receive Medicare and Medicaid coverage in the facility?
- Does the facility require residents to buy private insurance or participate in a special group insurance program for residents?
- What are the criteria and procedures for determining when a resident needs to be transferred from one unit to another? Who is involved in these decisions?
- What rights do residents have to participate in facility management and decision-making?
- How are complaints handled?
- On what grounds can residents' contracts or leases be terminated against their wishes?
- What other rules and policies cover day-to-day operation of the facility?
- Does the contract release the facility from any liability for injury to a resident resulting from negligence by the facility or third parties? Such waivers should be avoided.

Nursing Home Care

At the opposite end of the spectrum from the Sun Belt–style senior living community is the nursing home, an institution that provides skilled nursing care and related services, as well as rehabilitation services for the injured, disabled, and sick.

Only about 5 percent of Americans age sixty-five and older live in nursing homes at any given time, but researchers estimate that older Americans have about a 40 percent chance of spending at least some time in a nursing home. While some nursing home residents stay for extended periods, the majority stay in such a facility less than six months.

If you need to choose a nursing home for yourself or a loved one, you'll want to ask many of the same questions you would about a continuing-care retirement community (see above). In addition, you'll want to be aware of the legal rights of residents, which are particularly important given the institutional character of the nursing home environment.

Many people dread the prospect of living in a nursing home because of the loss of privacy and dignity. Be aware, though, that people don't check their rights and privileges at the door when they enter a nursing home. Although institutional care by its nature substantially limits one's lifestyle and scope of privacy, one should nevertheless expect high-quality, compassionate, and dignified care from nursing facilities.

The federal Nursing Home Reform Amendments of 1987, and corresponding state laws, protect residents in nearly all nursing facilities. For residents who lack capacity, the resident's agent under a power of attorney for health care or another legal surrogate recognized by state law (typically a family member) may exercise the resident's rights.

Federal law requires that nursing homes meet tough basic standards for the quality of life of each resident and for the provision of services and activities. Under the Basic Quality of Life Standard for Nursing Homes, every nursing facility must "care for its residents in such a manner and in such an environment as will promote maintenance or enhancement of the quality of life of each resident." The Basic Service and Activities Standard requires each nursing facility to "provide services and activities to attain or maintain the highest practicable physical, mental, and psychosocial well-being of each resident in accordance with a written plan of care which . . . is initially prepared with participation to the extent practicable of the resident or the resident's family or legal representative."

The federal Older Americans Act requires every state to operate a long-term-care ombuds program. The ombudsman is responsible for advocating on behalf of residents of nursing homes and other long-term-care facilities, such as assisted-living or board-and-care facilities. The ombuds staff provides education on long-term-care options and residents' rights, and investigates and resolves complaints made by or on behalf of residents.

Most states operate local or regional programs with local paid or volunteer ombuds staff. Residents and family members often find these go-betweens to be essential partners in resolving problems. Federal law requires nursing homes to allow the ombudsman access to residents and access to resident records. In addition, the ombudsman usually has special authority under state law to inspect records and take other steps necessary to respond to complaints.

Specific rights guaranteed by federal and state law include the following:

- **Information rights.** Nursing homes must provide:

  Written information about residents' rights.

  Written information about the services available under the basic rate and any extra charges for extra services.

  Advance notice of changes in room assignment or roommate.

  Upon request, latest facility-inspection results and any plan of correction submitted to state officials.

  Explanation of the resident's right to make a health care advance directive—i.e., power of attorney for health care or living will—and facility polices on complying with advance directives.

  Information about eligibility for Medicare and Medicaid and the services covered by those programs.

- **Self-Determination Rights.** Each resident has the right to:

Participate in an individualized assessment and care planning process that accommodates the resident's personal needs and preferences.

Choose a personal physician.

Voice complaints without fear of reprisal and receive a prompt response.

Organize and participate in resident groups (such as resident councils) and family groups.

- **Personal and Privacy Rights.** Residents have the right to:

Participate in social, religious and community activities as they choose.

Privacy in medical treatment, accommodations, personal visits, written and telephone communications and meetings of resident and family groups.

Confidentiality of personal and clinical records.

Access to the long-term-care ombudsman, one's physician, family members, and reasonable access to other visitors subject to the resident's consent.

Freedom from physical and mental abuse, corporal punishment, and involuntary seclusion.

Freedom from any physical restraint or psychoactive drug used for purposes of discipline or convenience, and not required to treat the resident's medical symptoms.

Protection of residents' funds held by the facility with a quarterly accounting.

- **Transfer and Discharge Rights.**

Residents may be transferred or discharged only for the following reasons:

- —The health, safety, or welfare of the resident or other residents requires it.
- —The nonpayment of fees.

—Improvement of the resident's health so that he or she no longer needs nursing home care.

—Closure of the facility.

Normally residents must receive at least thirty days' advance notice of a transfer or discharge, with information about appealing the transfer and how to contact the state long-term-care ombudsman program. The facility must prepare and orient residents to ensure safe and orderly transfer from the facility.

- **Protection Against Medicaid Discrimination.** Nursing homes must:

  Have identical policies and practices regarding services to residents regardless of the source of payment. (However, be aware that not all facilities participate in Medicaid.)

  Provide information on how to apply for Medicaid.

  Explain the Medicaid "bed-hold" policy—that is, how many days Medicaid will hold the resident's bed, or ensure priority readmission, after temporary absences.

  Not request, require, or encourage residents to waive their rights to Medicaid.

  Not require a family member to guarantee payment as a condition of a resident's admission or continued stay.

  Not "charge, solicit, accept, or receive gifts, money, donations, or other considerations" as a precondition for admission or continued stay for persons eligible for Medicaid.

What if you think a nursing home is not providing adequate care or respecting your rights or those of your loved one? That depends on the circumstances, but the following steps should help resolve most cases. The order may vary depending on the problem:

- Keep a log of the relevant details, including dates and personnel involved.
- Try to resolve the problem informally by talking to supervising staff.

- Many facilities have active resident councils or family councils. Bring the problem before these groups.

- Contact your long-term-care ombudsman.

- Contact the state regulatory agencies that license, certify and survey nursing homes. Usually, the state department of health has this responsibility.

- Contact a community legal assistance program, other advocacy organization, or private attorney experienced in long-term-care issues.

WHERE TO GET MORE INFORMATION

■

NEARLY EVERY STATE HAS federal information centers where information on federal services, programs, and regulations is available to consumers. Check the Yellow Pages of your local telephone directory for the office nearest to you. Your local library also can be a good source of helpful, free information. Various nonprofit agencies, such as the Better Business Bureau (BBB), can help you get more information on your legal rights and obligations in owning property. Look in your local telephone directory for your closest BBB office.

The federal government publishes a listing of many free or low-cost pamphlets on home ownership and home buying, including information on such topics as asbestos, pesticides, home-equity loans, mortgage refinancing, and reverse mortgages, among many others. This listing can be obtained from the Consumer Information Center-N; P.O. Box 100; Pueblo, CO 81002; 719-948-3334, fax 719-948-9724.

In addition, the Federal Trade Commission offers free publications on homes and real estate. Write to Public Reference, Federal Trade Commission, 6th and Pennsylvania Avenue, N.W., Washington, D.C. 20580, for a listing of what is available.

INDEX

INDEX